Hildegard W.
Messenbaugh, MD

Getting Even
A Manual
for Healing
Childhood
Trauma

THIRD WAY CENTER
PO Box 61385
Denver, CO 80206
www.thirdwaycenter.org

Designed by Hans Teensma, www.impressinc.com
Printed by The Studley Press
Cover art by William Matthews

ISBN: 978-1-4951-6135-3

Printed in the United States of America

Contents

Acknowledgments

BECAUSE THIS MANUAL has taken so many years to develop, there have been many people in my life who contributed invaluable information and help in the process. Without their input, effort, and encouragement, I could never have completed this work. Their continuous willingness to experiment with this method, their courage in implementing it, and their wisdom in giving critical feedback have made this manual a work in progress and will continue to make it grow.

Foremost, I want to thank the Board of Directors of Third Way Center for their persistence, patience, and support in making me complete this work. William Matthews, in his long years of dedication to Third Way Center and as president of its Board of Directors, has consistently been willing to let me try my hand at writing all this down, while pushing me to codify and organize the material we had been teaching and practicing at Third Way for many years. Without his persistence, I doubt that I would have undertaken this task, much less seen it through.

As I began the task, however, I recognized how much help I would need from our wonderful senior staff. Ms. Renee Johnson, then clinical director and now program director at Third Way Center; her then assistant clinical director and now clinical director, Kristi Edmonds; and the treatment leaders of all the houses have spent a great deal of their own time reading and rereading the many drafts of this manual, making corrections and suggestions, until it finally reached completion. They talked to their treatment staff about the treatment manual and began the process of teaching this method of trauma recovery. Extra-special thanks go out to them for their dedication. They have convinced not only our clients, their families, and our entire staff, but also countless caseworkers, client managers, guardians ad litem, and courts, that this method of trauma resolution is superior to previously employed treatment methods because it allows our clients and their families to be set free to pursue their destiny without being hindered by the effects of childhood trauma.

I want to thank my partner, David Eisner, the executive director at Third Way Center, who has worked with me for over thirty-five years to build Third Way Center with its dedicated staff, making this entire endeavor possible. I also thank my husband, Bert, for his endless gift of time and understanding. Without that, this book would never have gotten beyond the stage of being just another good idea.

And finally, I want to thank my wonderful, understanding, patient, and highly skilled editor, Michael Carr, for all he has done to help make the material I presented to him readable, enjoyable, and, ultimately, understandable.

*A mind once stretched by a new idea
never regains its original dimensions.*

—*Oliver Wendell Holmes, Jr.*

Preface

IN THE FIELD OF PSYCHOTHERAPY, "trauma" has become the catchword of the day. Of course, we have long known that trauma is bad for you and can cause immeasurable damage. People can traumatize each other in infinite ways. And so can nature and random events, mangling the psyche and changing forever the course of someone's life. And yet, lots of healthy individuals seem to be managing their lives just fine despite what appears to be unimaginably severe trauma. They seem to have drawn the lucky genes and the lucky set of environmental factors in the lottery that is life. They were the resilient children.

But some traumas are not surmountable even to the healthiest person, let alone to those less fortunate, who started with biological and environmental handicaps long before trauma tested their mettle. To them, trauma becomes insurmountable, particularly if it comes in the form of child sexual abuse—the breaking of boundaries between child and parent or primary caregiver. Oedipus knew it when he found out he had been sleeping with his mother. It ruined his life, to put it mildly, and he didn't know what to do about it except to gouge out his eyes and mourn eternally. Freud knew it a hundred years ago, when he treated Dora for only a few weeks and then wrote and lectured about her for years. He knew what was wrong with her and what had made her nonfunctioning—he just didn't know what to *do* about it. He pored over her story, went through every little detail of her trauma, and painstakingly connected it to every one of her self-destructive acts, over and over again, perhaps desensitizing himself to the horror of it all in the process. Maybe, eventually, it even helped him formulate his theory on sexual trauma and its devastating effects on people.

That was 1900. And ever since, we've been basically doing the same thing. Countless analysts during the twentieth century followed that example, and untold thousands of patients did their time on the couch, hoping for relief. It seemed for some that the analysis made their pain, their wounds, easier to bear. It never resolved their trauma, though. Then therapists noticed the seeming futility of this approach and gave up trying to deal with trauma. Instead, we invented a whole slew of new theories that said essentially, "Too bad that awful things have happened to you. What you must do is learn to control yourself, no matter what else might be handicapping you and preventing you from doing well. Now, shape up and correct your faulty thinking!" By "control yourself," we sometimes meant thought processes, sometimes feelings, and sometimes behavior. Whichever way we meant it, society intended that the victim should "suck it up"; "put the pain behind you"; "after all, it's in the past."

Somewhere along the line, we also decided that we should punish the people who inflicted these traumas on others. Actually, we have known for a long time that this was right and just, and we made more and more laws to punish perpetrators (provided that we caught them or wanted to catch them). The young perpetrators were easier to catch than the older, more sophisticated ones, and so the jails filled—especially the juvenile jails. But still, by the second half of the twentieth century, there were people who not only noticed and cared about the victims but also wanted to do something about the problem. That is, they were not interested solely in punishing the perpetrators. One of these people was Henry C. Kempe, MD.

I had the tremendous good fortune to be a pediatric intern at the University of Colorado Health Sciences Center when the renowned Dr. Henry Kempe chaired the Department of Pediatrics there. During that internship year, two babies came into the hospital who were the product of incest—same mother, same perpetrator (the father of the mother). Both babies died of multiple congenital malformations. God help us, we interns called the babies "blue maxes"—"blue" because they were always arresting and nearly dying all the time, and I don't know where the "max" came from. There was no agency to report this to, no case-worker to involve, no police report to make. I include this story only to illustrate how helpless we all were barely fifty years ago. It was during that time that Dr. Kempe started his pioneering work on determining just how destructive the sexual abuse of children really was. I want to underscore how important it was that the law also stepped in where we in the health care field could not. Indeed, we didn't know what to do about any of it.

And as we realized that juveniles were just as likely as adults to be the perpetrators of sexual abuse, someone came up with the idea of making them pay back to society what they had taken. And with that, the field of treating *all* offenders came into being. And a little later, the term "restorative justice" was born. The idea was both brilliant and fair: if you harm society, you must make amends! Again, it was at least a step forward in addressing the profound injustice being done by some people to others, the "others" being mostly children.

For over forty years, I have worked with teenagers. All of them had had brushes with the law, and most of them had offended greatly against society, and in the first few years, I tried to get them to pay back. But without a jail and without burly guards to make them, they mostly refused. Some just rebelled outright, but some had the courage to tell me why they refused. They wanted to know why they had to pay when the people who had abused them did not. Why must children pay for the injustices they were inflicting on others, when the adults who had perpetrated the same offenses on them—and from whom they had learned those very behaviors—did not have to pay any sort of restorative justice? Was it not a well-known fact that adults must always go first and set an example? Were *they* not the ones who had started the whole chain of injustices? It seemed a fair question. It was a new idea that stretched my mind, and a question that deeply affected me because it was the central question of my own life.

My life began shortly before the Second World War. I was born into a world of privilege and ease, with a wonderful family who had been successful and prospered for generations on the steppes of Hungary. Educated, isolated, and privileged, no one ever dreamed that this could all come crashing down. Then one night, in the spring of 1944, our neighbor's maid killed the entire family because they had a German surname. Then the Bolsheviks arrived, and ethnic cleansing began in earnest. That night, my family fled. First, we went to Budapest. The Soviets started bombing the city, and there was no water or electricity, and the advancing troops were sending German-surnamed people to the mines in Russia, so we fled again. Thinking of ourselves as Germans even though we had lived in Hungary and Yugoslavia for over two centuries, we thought to flee to Austria. After enduring many detours, bombings, endless crowds of refugees, hunger, and cold, we arrived in Austria. But instead of giving us safe haven, the Nazis declared us mongrels of mixed blood because, yes, the family had intermarried with Hungarians and Jews. They declared us "stateless and displaced persons." Since we were displaced, all right, and belonged to no one, they could do with us as they wished. And they decided that given the shortage of resources, the best thing was to eliminate us as soon as possible, in the gas chambers. When they ran low on the cyanide gas agent, they put us into railroad cattle cars and hauled us through the countryside, abandoning us, without shelter, food, or clothes, at various villages along the way. And so I grew up in a tiny Austrian village called Saalfelden am Steinernen Meer—a place none of us had heard of, could find on the map, or could even pronounce. We had no food, no shelter, no resources. It was Europe's coldest winter in decades. We lived in the gym of the local school and begged for food. In the spring, we boiled wild spinach, and we survived by the kindness of the local population. But my family never forgot the profound injustice of it all, and they never forgot to look for some form of retribution. Getting our former status back, they decided, would prove that the Nazis had not been able to destroy us as they wished. We would go on and then we would "get even" by getting all our status and our wealth back. The entire family was committed to that goal. It was not so much about revenge as about restoring balance in the family's life—taking back that balance, which had been disturbed against our will. In many trips back to Germany and Austria, it was vitally important to my family that "those people" should acknowledge and be astonished at our success.

Since I grew up all my life believing and living the principle of restorative justice, my young clients' questions about why the people who had wronged them never had to pay struck a deep note in me. I came to understand that restorative justice is not only what the perpetrator must pay. It is also what the *victim* must *get*. In my own case, I could not reach the perpetrators personally, and yet, the *restorative* part of my justice was something my entire family and I could accomplish! I had seen my family suffer and struggle with the trauma of being displaced, hurt, reviled, hunted, and starved. And though the term "post-traumatic stress disorder" had not yet been coined, I surely saw all the symptoms. And I understood that the trauma caused agonizing feelings that the victims often acted out with tears and anger.

So in some sense, I had always understood that a person's behavior did not just come out of the blue. Later on, as a psychiatric resident, I saw that even in psychosis the behavior made some sense to the person behaving in a certain maladaptive way. I also knew that the behavior often seemed incomprehensible and senseless to me. And often, to my amazement, the client knew that, too. My clients just did not seem to have any other choices. I knew that their actions always had *affect* attached to them—powerful emotions that drove the behavior. Having been a dutiful student of the psychoanalytical school, I also believed that something bad had happened to make them feel the way they did, which in turn made them act in troublesome ways. I just didn't know what to do about it. As it turned out, I didn't have to.

In the early 1990s, I had a young woman client who had been sexually abused by her biological father. I listened week after week to her pouring out her anger and the gruesome details of her abuse and her rage toward him, her mother, and the world. I empathized. I felt deeply sorry for her. I had the entire family in for treatment—without the biological father, I might add, since my client's "new" family seemed so healthy. Stepfather, mother, and the other siblings were functioning successfully and happily. And yet, I could not help my client. After too many weeks of getting nowhere, out of frustration I asked her one day, "Well, what do you want to *do* about it?"

That day, restorative justice was born to me. It was a new idea that changed the course of my life, and here is how: To my astonishment, out poured several years' worth of dreams and fantasies and wishes—some well thought out, others a jumble, and all of them secretly held. *I* may not have known what to do about her trauma, but *she* had certainly thought about it long and hard. The 7-year-old that this trauma, this injustice, had happened to had never stopped talking to her, no matter how much she tried to silence or outgrow the child. I realized, also, that I was stuck with sorting out all those thoughts that the 7-year-old was pouring out. Moreover, I would have to help my 17-year-old client see what was possible and what was not, and how to respond to the 7-year-old victim within her. I had initially thought that none of the retribution the 7-year-old had wanted all those years was possible, but I was deeply mistaken. My 17-year-old client ended up going to her church and telling the congregation that one of their members was a sexual perpetrator. And she made me go with her. It began her process of healing. She taught me that it was a process that went from acknowledging the bad behavior that had brought her to my office, to seeing that this behavior was driven by her deeply held angry feelings. These feelings were, by the way, the feelings of the 7-year-old victim, not the adolescent. I understood that it was the victimization itself that had brought all this about. But she knew enough to understand that this might sound like just an excuse for her bad behavior. And she knew that she wanted—no, absolutely *had*—to do something about it to solve her problem and get rid of the feelings and memories that plagued her.

She taught me a way to treat trauma—a way that involved six steps, six progressions, six boxes. It went from behavior to feelings that drove that behavior, to the underlying trauma, to the decision to actually do something about that unforgiven and unforgiving trauma. Only then did her feelings change profoundly. Some changed for the better because she felt she had actually taken charge of her life and stood up for herself. And some feelings changed in ways unanticipated by her or the family, because until then, not everyone understood why she had done what she did to "get even." But with *taking action* came a new set of behaviors, new self-confidence, and then even great forgiveness toward her perpetrator. She taught me that it took six very distinct phases to move on from being an acting-out victim to being a new person, free to resume control over one's life. In this way, the "six boxes" were born. Initially, I drew merely six sections or boxes, one on top of another: starting with *behavior* in box 1, leading to box 2, *feelings,* which pushed and drove box 1. Underneath was box 3, *trauma*—the cause of the content in boxes 2 and 1. But my client had taught me that it took another box, box 4, *justice*—the *doing something about* the trauma. It was that justice in box 4 that then led to box 5: the appearance of a whole set of *new feelings*. And this and only this would lead to box 6, *new behavior.*

A client thus begins with accepting that bad behavior begets punishment, failure, and pain. That behavior is driven by feelings. Behavior is always accompanied by strong, driving feelings. And the feelings? They come from *somewhere,* usually deep trauma. But then comes the question in box 4: what are you going to *do* about it? Humans need to be heard, to find justice. But nothing in life is free. Once we get justice, it brings with it a host of new problems and feelings. Hence box 5. Only when this is resolved does new behavior emerge.

Over the following years, I practiced this and had the good fortune to work with many gifted therapists, most of whom were brave and willing to think "outside the box," so to speak. Over time, we refined and modified this process until it was our clients who named it the "Six Boxes" rather than the "six steps toward getting well." It became a visual aid, a pathway that all adolescents—even those with limited intellects—seem able to follow and comprehend. Justice, fairness, "getting your say," standing up for yourself—all are truly cherished notions to all adolescents. And maybe not just to adolescents.

On November 18, 2012, I was watching CBS's *60 Minutes* when reporter Lesley Stahl presented a study by Kiley Hamlin and Karen Wynn of Yale University's Infant Cognition Center. Two groups of infants, aged 3 months and 6 months, watched two different puppet shows. In the first show, a puppet was trying to open a trunk while another puppet kept slamming the lid shut, preventing the trunk from being opened. Then someone who did not know which was the "good" puppet and and which was the "bad" puppet presented both puppets to each child. The infants from both groups overwhelmingly preferred the "good" puppet. That such young babies could make this distinction was amazing, but the second study was downright astonishing.

In the second study, the same scenario was played out in the puppet show, but this time, a third puppet came along and punished the "bad" puppet. When shown all three puppets, the infants overwhelmingly preferred not the "good" puppet but the *punishing* puppet. The 6-month-olds reached for that puppet and smiled broadly at it. And the group of 3-month-olds voted with their eyes by staring for a long time at the punishing puppet. It clearly seemed to support my notion that justice is what we all seek.

I then remembered an article in the May 5, 2010, *New York Times,* by Paul Bloom of the Yale University Infant Cognition Center, in which he talked about this study. He said, "Justice demands the good be rewarded and the bad punished." He discussed how this may indeed show that seeking justice is an inborn trait rather than a learned behavior. This goes against most previous stances by philosophers such as Rousseau and Locke who believed children to be savage beasts.

Not just infants and adolescents seek justice and need to learn how to achieve it. So do adults. Even staff, too, have to practice getting justice, with little traumas as well as big ones. And when we realize that even a minor "trauma," such as being treated rudely by a waitress, rankles with most people, we realize how poorly the human psyche takes to injustice, because even with such a minor, insignificant upset, we go home thinking of all the things we could and should have said to get even. Sometimes, some of us even do, such as leaving a penny as a tip in retribution for the insult. Imagining the chagrin it will cause makes us now "all even." Then, of course, comes that bit of guilt over it, and the promise to be a better person!

The concept of evenness, of balance, has existed throughout time. The ancient Egyptians had a concept called *ba'at,* in which all right and wrong was weighed on a scale, and after death that scale had to balance.

Taoists refer to something similar as *yin and yang*. Deeply religious people believe that God is the ultimate distributor of justice, and some have the concept of hell, where all the people who do wrong to us and to others will go to be punished. And we have even invented—and only reluctantly discarded—the concept of purgatory, where redemption is possible through suffering. And best of all, we have come to see the value in the concept of penance. The boxes are about all that, reduced to a mundane drawing, a stepwise process—a path to righting things for the children we have required penance from without offering them the same.

Although getting some justice for wrongs done is at the heart of the healing process, it was also clear from the beginning that much preparatory work had to go into this. This is what my patient taught me so many years ago, setting me on a new course. I knew her extremely well, and in the process of getting her life and family history, we formed an alliance. And that is what made the question I put to her answerable. And it was because I knew *what* was wrong that she answered honestly, trustingly, about what she wanted to do. But there was much more to this. First, I needed answers to these questions: (1) Who in her environment could help us get justice? And (2) what in her makeup, in her background, made it possible to choose the right form of justice? Only then could we make possible the restorative piece of justice: her going and confronting her perpetrator directly. The questions of who and what could help us had been answered in the process of history taking.

Of course, there was also the issue of who and what would *hinder* this process. In the course of the preparatory work, this became apparent. Mother and stepfather were fearful and hesitant about her wish to confront her perpetrator. This had to be dealt with. So did her ADHD, which not only made her more vulnerable to the trauma but also made confrontation impossible until she was stabilized on the right medication. But it was the airing of all issues—the clear diagnosis, which the client and the family perceived as being the "whole, unvarnished truth"—that initially came as a great relief to the entire family. Then, when there was hope that, by an action, their daughter might move on and grow up normally, this allowed everyone in the family to engage in the process of restoring the balance in her life. Thus, as stated in Third Way Center's motto, truth and hope were also born. Truth consisted of knowing what the problem really was, and hope meant that something could actually be done about the problem, which would set her free and let her grow up. Since then, this has increasingly become the cornerstone for Third Way Center's treatment philosophy.

To systematize this process for the therapist, we surrounded the six boxes in an envelope of six "bins"—six categories of knowledge about the client. The bins hold the knowledge of who the client is as a total human being: the client's past and present and all the people in the client's life. All the significant people and all the significant events in the client's life should become evident through this process, either by what is being said or by what is missing in the inquiry. The whole drawing began to look like an avocado to me, and the image has stuck. And in some ways, this has become a metaphor for the process, with the outside—the flesh of the avocado—feeding the large central core, or kernel, from which a new tree can emerge. The historical information feeds the therapeutic process. It's all so easy to remember, yet difficult to see through, as we will discuss when we come to each section. (Please see Appendix 1, which shows the six bins and six boxes as presented to the client, the family, and the treatment team.)

INTRODUCTION

Taking a History:
The Six Bins

LIKE ALL SUCCESSFUL ENDEAVORS, the treatment process begins with the preparatory work. Therapy is like a military campaign: it takes a lot of planning. And as with any campaign, the better and more detailed the knowledge of the terrain, the more likely success will be. Both God and the devil are in the details, and nowhere more than in the work it takes to get through the six boxes, the stepwise process for trauma recovery. The more you know about your client, the easier it will be. Put this way, it makes such easy sense. It makes sense, for example, that we need to know where the trauma began, who the support systems are, and even what language and what imagery the therapist needs to use. It makes sense that filling all six bins with as much data as possible—even continuing to add data during the treatment process itself—is not only valuable but mandatory. One would never think of invading a country without knowing what one was likely to find there that might help or hinder the invasion. What comes to mind is the First Gulf War, when we invaded the Arabian Desert with North American troops who were not dressed for the 120-degree heat.

And yet, when the therapist is presented with an acting-out, deeply hurt, angry client and a worn-out, defensive family, the temptation is to jump right into the middle of the healing process—without the slightest idea where it all will lead.

Recently, I met with client M and his family. They all were terribly angry and hostile to the therapeutic process. Since getting a history was so difficult, we asked them just to bring in all the paperwork they had accumulated during the long years of previous therapists and placements from Texas to Colorado. They brought in a crate stuffed full of papers. Starting with M's adoption from a small village east of Moscow, Russia, it included discharge summaries from treatment centers, police contacts, school testing, and so on. I spent the entire Memorial Day weekend reading through all the material. During the next several weeks, the father tested me repeatedly to gauge whether I had actually read the material. Only when he was convinced that I had did he share with me the fact that *no one* had ever asked him for this historical material. In fact, during one of M's placements in another center, the psychiatrist there actually yelled at the mother for drinking during the pregnancy with M, since he clearly showed all the symptoms of fetal alcohol syndrome. She blithely told the doc that she had indeed been drinking on many occasions before, during, and after M's pregnancy, which further infuriated him. Finally, her husband had had enough. "You jackass!" he said. "Our son is adopted, which you would know if you had troubled yourself to read even one single note from his history!" All further treatment ended there.

The temptation is even greater when therapists do not know their own history and are afraid to look at their own trauma issues. This, coupled with the prevailing trend of training therapists exclusively in quick fixes—motivational interviewing therapies, cognitive behavioral therapy to fix "faulty thinking," client-centered therapy, problem-focused therapy, and so on—makes most therapists woefully ill equipped or flat-out unwilling to go through this crucial first step in trauma treatment. The truth is, these therapeutic models are often tremendously helpful and come into play in the trauma treatment method used at Third Way Center, as we will see in later chapters. As the great historian Arnold J. Toynbee pointed out, "He who refuses to learn from history is doomed to repeat it." This is true for clients, therapists, and families, and it remains the greatest source of countertransference encountered in the treatment process.

And, of course, we have, from caseworkers, client managers, and all secondary payers, the pressure of limited time allotted by the system for this process. This makes it tempting just to go back to old methods of treatment, learned and practiced for years, rather than start at the beginning by taking a thorough history, painstakingly going over every last detail to be sure *all* aspects of the client become known. It is also easier, and tremendously tempting, just to accept what others have said or written about the client and what goals "the system" has for the client. By "the system," I mean Social Services and the juvenile justice system, although these do indeed have much information to add to the history! But they must never become the sole source of information on the client's history, especially since previous treatment has not been successful. If it had been, the client would not be at Third Way Center. The other source of pressure, of course, comes from the clients themselves. The suffering and years of treatment they have endured have brought them to such depths of despair that they simply *know* that this therapist, too, like all the others, will not know anything whatever and certainly will not know how to deal with their trauma or what to do about it. And since the trauma—the injury done to the client—often appears painfully obvious, it's enormously tempting to jump right in and offer hope about what can be done to get justice. But years of sometimes painful experience has taught me that such a strategy leads only to an endless morass and blind alleys, causing further pain and disappointment to the client and more frustration for the therapist.

Most clients, families, and outside treatment teams are curious about why the history has to be taken at all. It seems unreasonable to them to have to watch the therapist struggle with getting it all right, getting all the family members straight, wanting to know all the details of previous events and the seemingly tedious details of daily life. The client and the family have had to wander through this psychological terrain so many times already, with no clear reason why, that it will help if we explain to them the reason for our curiosity. This question needs to be asked of ALL the participants in the healing process: "Can everyone agree that the client has been traumatized and that nobody just decides to screw up their life on purpose?" And once we get everyone's agreement on that, then it's time to take a brief overview of the Six Boxes to Healing Trauma.

We need to take the overview now because, without the history-taking process, we can't answer two vitally important clusters of questions:

- What is wrong? What dysfunction is here? What happened to cause this profound dysfunction within the client and the family? That is the diagnostic part: the why, how, and what went wrong, and what is impairing the client and the family.

- What strength within the client and the family can help the healing process? Who in the family can and will help the client recover and can make the healing process possible?

At Third Way Center, we're a bit luckier than most places in starting this venture, since many of our clients have been in anywhere from eight to fifty placements or even more. So the paper trail of failed therapies is long indeed. Thus, we know a lot of things that *don't* work, and knowing this, we can at least make fresh mistakes and not repeat the old ones. Also, innumerable details of our clients' lives are already recorded, even though much of this may have changed over the years and may be incorrect. Still, it's helpful to know the avenues, previously explored in therapy and placements, that have failed. It helps to know what misconceptions and untruths have been pursued. But most of all, it's important to know that a lot of other smart, kind people have looked at our client before and studied the case, so at least one or two must have made observations or collected data that was not pursued but that turns out to be valuable, crucial, even pivotal. The chart the client brings always contains nuggets that are worth remembering and documenting. The old charts, therefore, are a significant beginning and have lots of data—data that must be collected, read, and sorted into the bins. Then and only then does the direct process of gathering history from the client, family, and treatment team (such as client managers and case workers) begin. To get usable information takes careful reading and sorting. To make matters a bit easier, it's helpful (though not entirely traditional) to review this material with the client and let them help the therapist check out the accuracy of what you find.

> **Example:** C had been a client at Third Way Center for several months, struggling to meet the demands of the program. He had acted out repeatedly, always maintaining that he was "a really bad person" and that this explained his troublesome behavior. The treatment staff believed that his mother's suicide when he was 3, and the subsequent dissolution of his family, was the trauma that haunted him. He believed that he was the cause of his mother's suicide because she had had severe postpartum depression after his birth—or so the family said—and that therefore, it was all his fault. Since nothing seemed to help him, we decided to go back and redo the history. As we reviewed once again

and reread the chart and all previous notes, two significant pieces of information gradually emerged: (1)
the death certificate never said it was a suicide, only
that it was an accidental overdose with Elavil; and (2)
C himself had asked several times how much Elavil it
took "to kill yourself" and had wrongly been told "a lot,"
thus convincing him even more that it was a suicide
(though the mother had not left a suicide note). When
he could perceive that maybe, even probably, she had
accidentally overdosed after drinking heavily and that
the death was also connected with several severe fights
she had had with adult family members, it opened up
entirely new therapeutic avenues for C.

So after reevaluating the previous therapies comes the tedious
process of seeing and asking as many people as possible who have ever
known the client their version of the truth and their version of the history. All this requires critical listening. By this, I mean that as the data
is collected, it has to be sorted into categories that are comprehensible
to the therapist and practicably viewable in one reading. "Critical" does
not mean judgmental. "Critical" also does not mean either believing
or not believing. "Critical" means believing everything and believing
nothing, merely taking it to be "data", data that needs to be organized
into the bins. During the entire process of reading data and eliciting
information from client, family, caseworkers, client managers, or who-
ever else has ever known the client, it's best to remember in the sorting
process the two groups of answers the therapist is hunting for: (1) what
is wrong, that is, the diagnosis for both client and family; and (2) the
strength and possible alliances available. Note: the question of what
will "heal" the client has not even been considered yet, since it cannot
be asked until strength and weakness—including structural weakness,

such as biological illnesses—have been found and an alliance has been forged during that process.

For that purpose, we have divided the history into six categories, which surround the six boxes. (See Appendix 2.) The six categories into which a person's history can be sorted present six areas that give the most complete picture of the client as a whole person that we can get before therapy can begin. For all practical purposes, it is easier to see these six areas as six bins where we can put pieces of information and knowledge bit by bit, as they are elicited, regardless of the order they come in. Having a copy of this always at hand makes it easier to remember the process, and it allows the therapist to make notes and sort information at the moment it comes. It is also a useful visual clue to what the therapist is overemphasizing and what the therapist is missing—for example, if one bin seems to include excessive information while another is nearly empty. On second review, it is often exactly that empty area of knowledge of the client's history that turns out to be the most significant, and the bins visually show how biased our information-gathering process really is.

Whereas the six boxes are the heart, or kernel, of the avocado, the six bins of the history are the meat—the sustenance of the process. The six bins are divided according to a simple system of thinking of a person (the client) as a whole human being. The same categorization applies to each family member. Thus, a human being is several things:

- a physical being with a specific physical and biological makeup
- a spiritual and cultural being
- a psychological being
- a member of a specific socioeconomic system
- a member of a specific family
- a person with a specific developmental history

It matters little in what order, or how systematically, those bins are filled. Much of it depends on the training of the therapist. Social workers tend to start with family systems or social issues, psychiatrists with body and psyche, pastorally trained therapists with the spiritual. Much of it depends on the specific interest of the individual therapist. It is easy to inquire and track and then get lost in the client's history according to the specific personal bias of the training that the therapist received. And it's easy to over- or underestimate the importance of one or another of the bins because of personal bias. Only by rigorously filling every one of the categories can these biases be minimized so that a more realistic picture of the client will emerge. It is most helpful, initially on meeting clients and families, simply to note what the therapist can hear, see, and smell. The immediacy of that material makes it the easiest place to start. My favorite fable includes the story of Parsifal, the perfect knight of the Arthurian Round Table, who found King Mark and the Holy Grail but was banished to wander forever, never to see the Grail again, simply because he had not had the empathy to ask the king, who was obviously wounded, how he had come by his wounds. I wonder how often our clients would like to banish us forever for the same reason!

> **Example:** E had been a client at Third Way Center for many months. She was an exemplary client, rarely causing problems, and when she did act out, she was always most apologetic. But she always remained sad, and when she acted out, it was always sexual in nature. After a while, her generally "good" behavior graduated her to a less restrictive program within Third Way Center. Still, she remained the same, behaving well for a long time, then acting out destructively against herself. The team decided to redo her history, especially her

sexual history. Much to everyone's astonishment, new history emerged about her parents' lifestyle as devoted hippies, dedicated to "free love," who believed that E should be part of their sex life because it was "natural." So from very early in her life, she had been exposed to sexual issues that scared and scarred her. New avenues of therapy emerged to get at what her trauma really was and where her possible "justice piece" lay. Because her family was cut off by having their rights terminated, the family bin was quite empty, and the assumption was that she knew little about them. This was grossly incorrect to begin with, for she had kept in secret contact with her family all along. We just hadn't asked her!

This example makes it clear that the information in the bins determines the process of the six boxes and makes it possible to go back for more information as obstacles appear in the healing process. When the therapeutic process falters or gets stuck, it is always possible to go back to the six bins to see where the clues or missing pieces of information might be. It also becomes clear that the process leads to the discovery of where the trauma lies, who caused it, and who is involved in it. It will often lead to the discovery of where the client's problematic behavior may have originated—that is, where they learned it.

Most important of all, the very process of getting all this information requires the therapist's deep personal interest and direct contact with both client and family. For this will form the therapeutic alliance necessary for the healing process to begin. In all the time I have been in practice, I have never met a person who did not want to be understood or who, in the long run, didn't like talking about him- or herself. Humans have a deep need and desire to be understood and to have their story heard and even recorded. Also, clients have an equally powerful aversion to the therapist's snap decision on what is "wrong"—no matter how obvious the trauma is or how obvious the symptoms of that trauma appear to be to the therapist or even to the entire treatment team. This is especially true at Third Way Center, where so many of our clients have recounted their trauma a hundred times and have had their symptoms pointed out to them—mostly with the request that the client immediately let go of the symptoms since the symptoms seem so maladaptive.

Unfortunately, it isn't possible for our clients to change their behavior and go from box 1 to box 6 in the way that it is for, say, my dog. I don't ask the history of my dog's bad behavior. I stop him—physically if necessary—and sternly say "NO," and he changes (though not always immediately). But people don't seem to respond like dogs. And neither people nor dogs turn their lives upside down with no purpose other than to make themselves miserable. Again, nobody screws up their life on purpose. As a matter of fact, acting out is specifically designed by the client to stop the very misery they find unbearable. Clients are deeply connected to their families, their past, their makeup. It is up to the therapist to help them set themselves free and to teach them the method for doing so—a method that they can apply all their lives, through *all* their troubles.

During the history-taking process, it is also most important for the therapist to refrain from being judgmental and, most of all, to avoid being unkind. Though people want to share their lives and their pain, they will do so only in a setting that is conducive (i.e., nonjudgmental and empathic). It is this empathy that makes the therapist find some commonality with the client and the family. And that commonality is particularly important in the treatment of adolescents, who, despite what they may say, care deeply that their therapists "like" them. Families, too, despite all the disapproval they have met with and no matter how angry they are when they arrive in therapy, want the therapist's nonjudgmental interest. Empathy is necessary if we are ever to sort through the many conflicting, often skewed views supplied to Third Way Center by the referring agencies. Therefore, all this material previously gathered can be both a boon to our knowledge about our client, and a disadvantage. Either way, when talking with the client and the family to take a more complete history and fill all six bins, it is important to remember that both the client and the family have given that history dozens of times. So the therapist, who is keeping the categories of the bins clearly in mind and has sorted all the information gathered from other sources, should not start out pretending to know nothing about the client or the family. That would at once feel false to the client and the family. Instead, the therapist should explain that she or he is going to check the veracity of the supposedly known information with them and ask about information that appears to be missing—that is, the unfilled or perhaps even empty bins.

Another important reason for getting as complete a history as possible is that research clearly shows that children with underlying structural defects, either physical or mental, are much more vulnerable than others to trauma and its damaging effects. For example, if a child has ADHD (like my client who first taught me about restorative justice), it will be helpful first to remove the symptoms of this vulnerability through proper medication *before* embarking on trauma treatment. The same is true for other common deficits such as closed head injuries, affective illnesses, unregulated diabetes, fetal alcohol syndrome, or fetal alcohol effect. Any of these structural defects might have to be addressed first with therapy, medication, or social interventions. Therapy might be psychopharmacological or involve physical alterations in a person's lifestyle. (Is it a defense mechanism that's holding up the process? Is it reckless lifestyle? Or is it a biologically determined handicap?) Or the structural defect might require several medications or social interventions, such as finding parents or significant others, before the client can deal with the trauma. A carefully taken history should reveal this more clearly.

> **Example: L**, a client at Third Way Center, was in the midst of successfully getting her restorative justice. Her mother, whom she had been separated from, had to be found since L needed and wanted mother's blessing. Her father, who was her abuser, was about to go to trial, and though she had resisted testifying against him initially, she had decided that going "to tell on him" in open court was indeed what she wanted to do once she got her mother's permission. But then the mother, who had severe liver problems, suddenly took a turn for the worse, and it appeared that she might soon die. Taking care of her seriously ill mother and making provisions for her handicapped older sister became the primary focus of L's therapy, before she could begin to deal with the upcoming trial. For L to testify, she first had to get her mother's permission, which she got only after standing by the mother until the mother recovered.

As L's case shows us, only after the client, the family, and all other significant persons such as caseworkers and client managers are known and understood as much as possible can therapy and the healing process begin. With a full, carefully taken and sorted history, the beginnings of an alliance between all parties involved should be taking shape. It is worth stressing again that no matter how well and how thoroughly the initial history was taken, sorted, and evaluated, throughout the entire treatment process new information will emerge that will alter that process. What the original history taking should accomplish is a way of knowing the client, the family, the previous treatment, and most of the trauma suffered—that is to say, a correct diagnosis. The six bins should provide the truth component in our treatment. Only then can we reasonably offer our clients the hope of overcoming trauma, and a path—the six boxes—to get them there.

In the case of the angry father with the adopted son from Russia, that long and involved history included some Russian birth records that clearly recorded severe encephalopathy at birth, and his biological mother's drinking, both of which left him with severely delayed frontal lobe development. This made him extremely impulsive, for example— a deficit that had to be addressed with medication *before* any psychological treatment for his cultural adjustment could begin.

Essentially, at the end of the diagnostic process, all parties need to be in agreement on what the trauma is, what the diagnosis is, and what and who can be helpful in the treatment process. When the therapists and either the family or the outside agencies are not in agreement on these points, therapy cannot proceed. As much as possible, everyone should agree to this, though it is amazing how often the therapist is the only one who seems to "know" what the diagnosis is, and has not shared or gotten agreement from the client, the family, or the treatment team. So it seems that this process is not as easy as it appears; otherwise, therapists wouldn't skip it so often.

> **Example:** J had been incarcerated for some time before being sent to Third Way Center for "emancipation skills." But during the history-taking process, it became abundantly clear that his severe early sexual abuse had not been dealt with (beyond simply acknowledging it). His outside agency team believed he had "successfully" overcome this through his previous cognitive behavioral therapy. Also, neither he nor they wanted to revisit that chapter of his past. Although that is not unusual,

in this case it was impossible to convince either the client or his agency team to relent. He got a job almost immediately and appeared to function well. He seemed driven and anxious, but at the urging and enthusiastic support of his outside treatment team, he poured all his energy into his job. As he became more and more exposed to the temptations of the outside world, he quickly reverted to drug use, and his probation was revoked. He ended up incarcerated again. Once he was free of incarceration, the old trauma had quickly resurfaced, and he had to self-medicate.

Thankfully, there are many more cases where the referring agency eventually (though often reluctantly) does give permission and lends support to the task of healing trauma rather than merely acknowledging it. Acknowledging the trauma and talking about it, knowing it, and having empathy with it seems not to be enough for people whose memories of events are too acute and lasting. And correcting the faulty thinking caused by the trauma may be helpful, but too often, it doesn't last and cannot erase those memories of the trauma. And never, in any of these treatments, does the victim get any justice.

Example: N was a young girl at Third Way Center who clearly had all the symptoms of fetal alcohol syndrome and had suffered severe neglect and abandonment, which was her trauma. How to present this to the parents became a major problem. When the first diagnosis came up in a staffing, mother, father, and stepmother all became quite angry and defensive. A heated discussion ensued over who did or did not drink and when everyone gave up drinking. In the midst of this, the mother announced she had to go to her alcohol recovery class and would have to cut our session short. There was silence in the room. When, after a few seconds, the treatment team was able to support her for those classes, it broke the stalemate, and we were then free to proceed with the diagnosis.

One other often overlooked source of history is the mental status exam. This test should always be administered by the primary therapist within the first week of treatment. (See Appendix 4.) Its sections will be discussed as the pertinent information that they provide fits into particular sections of the six bins. This test is most commonly administered to the client, but it is possible to give parts of it, such as the "family portrait," to various family members to fill out.

And so the process of taking a history begins and is divided into the following bins, or categories (as outlined in Appendix 2). This happens as part of the endeavor to look at the whole person and at the rest of the family members—physically, spiritually, culturally, psychologically, socioeconomically, developmentally, and, finally, as members of a sociological unit loosely known as the family.

At the end of this process, however, it should be possible for the therapist to make an imaginary movie of the client's life. It should be possible to cast the film with all the characters in the movie, to show their daily lives, to locate the people in time and space, and to know the motivations of all the principle actors. By this point, the working diagnoses should be reasonably clear and should be agreed on by the entire treatment team.

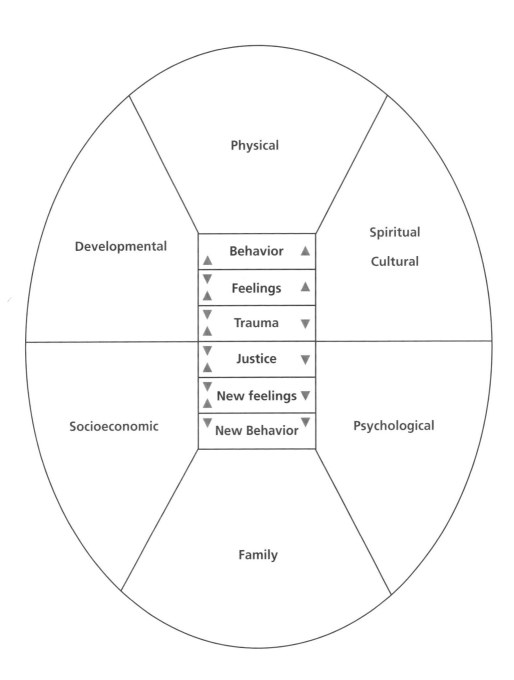

The Six Bins

BIN 1.

The Client and Family Members as Physical Beings

ALTHOUGH WE ALL KNOW not to *judge* a book by its cover, we can certainly glean from it a great deal about what lies inside. And because we are humans, we cannot help noting and deducing from physical appearances. So it is in our nature to start first with this method of gathering history.

Four aspects in the physical nature of humans need particular attention: *appearance, function, illnesses,* and *somatization.*

1. Appearance

The main thing here is for the therapist to become aware of what the senses are conveying—what the therapist can *see, hear,* or *smell.* Visual, auditory, and olfactory input from the client, the family, and even the referring agency team members (no one is safe) is the therapist's very first direct and verifiable data in the mosaic that will eventually become a complete portrait of the client and the family. It is also the easiest source for nonmedically trained therapists to overlook. Personal appearance can give the therapist many clues to the client's or the family's strengths and challenges. Here are some of the questions that appearance can answer:

A. Does the stated age appear correct? It matters greatly whether the client looks much older or much younger than the stated age. For example, people's expectations of clients who look much younger than the stated age are much lower than for clients who look much older than their stated age. Younger-looking clients evoke generally more empathy. The amount of empathy the therapist can or cannot muster often depends on nothing more substantial than the outward appearance of the client and the family. As unfair as it may seem, people whom other people perceive as good looking or "cute" get more empathic treatment, whether they deserve it or not.

B. How are they dressed? Are they dressed more or less in accordance with their age and status? Are they wearing a T-shirt with a particular saying on it? People, especially teens, often advertise their feelings and beliefs this way. It's a great entrée for a conversation with the client or the family about what the saying may or may not mean.

C. Is the client or the family extraordinarily tall, short, skinny, or fat? Do any of them have physical handicaps? What sort, and what is their origin? How have they handled their unusual physical attribute(s)? This may be hard to ask about since most therapists' mothers taught them middle-class good manners forbidding such questions.

D. Do you notice unusual features that might lead you to suspect a physical condition such as FAS, or a genetic condition such as fragile X syndrome?

E. Are they poorly groomed? And if so, why? Did they just come from a hard day's work, or do they always look like this?

F. Do they have tattoos? And if so, what do they say? Tattoos are marvelous advertisements of attachments and belief systems.

G. Do they smell of alcohol? Tobacco smoke? Marijuana? Once noted, we must ask about it, no matter how awkwardly it comes off when first attempted. Making the inquiry nonjudgmental, childlike, and gentle will make this possible.

H. What is their speech pattern, accent, and tone? What's the pitch of their voice?

These physical observations are often a good, more or less neutral point to start a session with adolescents in particular, but also with their families. If there is an eye-catching physical feature, whether natural or artificial, it must be addressed and noted immediately. Few adolescents can resist a discussion around this. As a matter of fact, I have never met a teen who could resist talking about an item of clothing or a saying on a T-shirt or a tattoo, even when they've just said they will not talk to a "therapist." Therapists, being for the most part people who have been brought up with traditional middle-class values, have the most difficulty with this aspect of history taking. They become judgmental and then freeze because they have been taught never to talk about obvious physical features, especially those they have learned to judge as being undesirable, such as a limp, scar, wound, birthmark, or confinement to a wheelchair. Here, as elsewhere in the process of taking a history, it is important merely to *note,* not to draw conclusions. For example, rather than drawing a conclusion about what appears to be a gang tattoo, ask about it. Therapists, like other humans, draw snap conclusions about other people, based on appearance. For example, as much research has shown, we often rate people or clients as more or less likable, and want to help them, depending on the way they look. This process of noting, commenting, exploring the physical aspects has to be repeated and noted with each family member.

> **Example:** When R was admitted to Third Way Center, the first encounter the therapist had was with the mother. She was wearing a tiny skirt, stiletto heels, and a blouse that revealed a lot of cleavage. The boys in the house could barely contain themselves. Our pointing out to the

mother that this made our jobs difficult led into a long discussion about what clothing does or does not say to our teenagers, and about the relationship she had with her son. It turned out to be a very seriously oedipal relationship. Bringing up the issue of her clothing also told the mother that the therapist would not be intimidated by any subject whatever and could talk to her kindly and with a sense of humor about it. It would be perfectly acceptable for the therapist even to admit that bringing this up was a bit embarrassing for both the client and the therapist but that it needed to be talked about. In this case, it first resulted in a bit of an argument but quickly led to the entire problematic issue in this family: the lack of boundaries between mother and son, which actually had traumatized this client.

2. Function

During the entire process of taking a history, it is important to note how the client functions physically. Is breathing difficult? How do they manage chairs, stairs, and doors? Are they restless and agitated? Calm? Lethargic? Wiggly? Tense? Relaxed? Sleepy? Sweaty? Smiling? Frowning? In other words, how does the client function or deal with the situation of the interview physically? And what clues are there physically to verify or demonstrate whether the affect matches what the client or the family is saying? For example, when a mother is recounting the bad behavior of her son, she may be smiling rather than showing concern. Or a client who says he is in great pain can still pay rapt attention to a conversation. Whenever we have physical signs that a physical condition might affect the process of the interview, we must deal with that aspect first and directly. Then, for the interview to continue, that condition needs to be alleviated as much as possible. A client with severe ADHD makes a poor historian, for example, so it might be more helpful to alleviate that symptom before proceeding with the history-taking process.

The observations also need to include where the client or family member sits, what arrangements they have chosen regarding their physical proximity to each other, and any contact or lack thereof between family members. The most difficult aspect of this is noting the contact, or lack of it, between the client or clients and the therapist. This is often left out because most of us therapists think that we know how lovable, kind, and approachable we are, and therefore, we assume that clients must undoubtedly feel the same about us. Alas, that is rarely the case, which makes sense considering the terrible experiences most of our clients have had with many of the caregivers they have known. So it is best to actually note whether they are having difficulties because the therapist is, say, female, gay, white, African American, and so on. Does the therapist represent all that is wrong with the social service system, and is the therapist therefore reaping the client's anger? It is important to clarify this early and as soon as it is noted from the behavior of the client or the family. That means it needs to receive top priority in the initial discussion and to be resolved as much as possible, even if it means that another therapist needs to take over.

> **Example:** When S was first seen at Third Way Center, the therapist assigned to him was a pretty, young-looking, middle-class female, whereas the family were blue-collar people from a big city on the East Coast. Initially, the family refused to give any history. They were extremely guarded until they discovered another male therapist, working in the same facility, who was originally from the same city they came from. They felt that he could relate much better to their particular

blue-collar background. It was hard not to be judgmental and to put the need of the client above the need of the therapist, but once the male therapist took over, it made history taking—and, of course, eventually, therapy—much easier. It was an issue not of gender but of commonality. Of course, it isn't always necessary to switch therapists. Sometimes, merely nondefensively discussing the matter or offering a switch can alleviate the problem and give the family the message that their preferences are heard and not judged.

As for gender issues; it's helpful to know and be able to approach this subject openly. Sexual functioning is one of the physical attributes that color and preoccupy adolescents in particular. Sexual identity, of course, is one of the major issues to be resolved during adolescence, and the family's reaction to this task is significant to both the teen and the therapist. Sexual functioning can best be approached with questions around significant others in the life of both the client and the family members. Sexual activity in the client's life often provides many clues to sexual trauma history, as do the sexual activities of family members. This is particularly important when a sexual abuse history has been previously reported or is suspected. Though these inquiries must be made, they require great skill and sensitivity on the part of the therapist. Supervision from an experienced therapist can be helpful.

3. Illness

The first two aspects of considering a client as a physical being require dispassionate but critical observation, whereas the next two sections require investigation. In training, when we were taught to ask clients how they are or how they feel, we likely forgot that this means not just emotionally but also physically. It matters greatly if the client has had to deal with physical illness. For example, in many cases, children who have undergone major invasive genitourinary procedures have shown symptoms mimicking those of sexual abuse. At Third Way Center, we have had a number of clients who, as children, suffered from illnesses requiring urinary-tract diagnostic procedures that the child perceived as excessively invasive. Ultimately, through further childhood trauma, the child came to perceive this as sexual abuse. Also, adolescent clients who have had to assist in the care of sick parents on a very intimate level sometimes have had what appeared to be sexual abuse issues. The same is true for children who have witnessed their significant caregivers' sexual acting out, whether auditorily or visually. They, too, have at times exhibited severe sexual abuse symptoms. Also, a child with physical illnesses is more vulnerable to trauma and often has fewer resources to fight off the effects of trauma.

If the client has an underlying biological mental illness, this makes dealing with trauma that much more difficult. If the client has underlying schizophrenia, for example, or severe chronic kidney disease, the effects of trauma are more severe. What may be manageable, in terms of trauma, to a resilient, healthy child may be overwhelming and completely debilitating to another who is less resilient and who may have to deal with underlying physiological deficits. This is true, for example, for children with ADHD. Also, the illnesses of the child client are often hereditary and of great significance in the family system. Therefore, it is important in the family meetings to inquire specifically about illnesses within the family system.

Concerning illness in the client or family, it is important to notice what the two tests for organicity on the mental status exam reveal. These two tests are the orientation questions and the drawings of the square, diamond, circle, and dots. (See Appendix 4, "Mental Status Exam.") With more and more research showing that repeated even minor closed head trauma causes significant impairment, it is important to follow up these mental status questions with a discussion with the client and the family about a possible history of closed head injuries, including, for example, those resulting from football impacts, gang fights (often overlooked), falls, vehicular accidents, and so on.

> **Example:** E was admitted to a Third Way Center facility because of violent, unmanageable fighting at a youth detention facility. A careful history taking determined that after he had a major closed head injury, he became a gang enforcer, thereby sustaining many more closed head injuries. He required extensive neurological testing and neurological follow-up.

4. Somatization

How do the client and the family perceive and deal with illnesses? In discussing individual and family illnesses, it is important to note the nature of the illness and how it may or may not be used as a way of expressing emotional content. For example, children with sexual abuse often complain of chronic abdominal pain. In some families, aches and pains may be more acceptable than complaints of a psychological nature, such as sadness or anger.

> **Example:** H came to Third Way Center having had innumerable medical tests and procedures during much of her childhood. She required an inordinate amount of care from her mother. H had been sexually abused by a former stepfather, whom the mother still had contact with, although much of the time, the client's illnesses had prevented the mother from seeing him. In another case, N's long chronic childhood illness had kept him the center of the family. He was pampered

by his caring, doting mother. But this made separation and facing the realities of adolescence difficult, and he had major separation issues. In both cases, it was the supposed chronic illness that served as a way of dealing with underlying traumatic issues.

For psychiatric illnesses, too, powerful outside forces often promote staying sick. Thus, the target organ or illness is often chosen symbolically as the source of the emotional pain. It is important to know this, because in the course of therapy, these symptoms will need attention and the correct interpretation from the therapist.

> **Example:** When T was first seen in therapy at Third Way Center, his mother firmly believed that all his acting out was a result of their house being haunted. The "bad emanations" from the house had caused his inability to function and all his PTSD symptoms. He was constantly "ill" with a great number of physical complaints, which the entire nuclear family attributed to the house and not to the mother's untreated severe childhood sexual abuse, which T was suffering from by proxy. Mother and son had an inordinately close relationship, and he had become a parentified child with the job of keeping a status quo that the family could tolerate.

This chapter contains a lot of information about what obstacles must be dealt with for the therapeutic work to be able to happen. The purely observational data collected will also allow the therapist to note where psychopharmacological interventions might be most useful during the treatment process.

But even more importantly, this chapter is about a picture being worth a thousand words. Because it is such a cornerstone of all that follows, here are some tips on how to make it work:

Therapists often get so involved in talking, they forget these three simple rules: *look, listen, smell.* And then remember what you saw, heard, and smelled. For the rest of the history-taking process, this will be your reality check for how well what the client and the family are saying matches the physical manifestations of affect. That is, does what you see, hear, and smell match the words?

When first meeting a client or family, spend a couple of minutes just observing them before you introduce yourself to them. Clear your mind of all the preoccupations that this job of being a therapist brings with it. Just look. Then introduce yourself and begin a socially innocuous conversation. I like talking about the weather. Everyone likes talking about it, and it's always too hot, too cold, too windy, too humid, too dry. Or traffic—everyone loves to complain about it. These are topics that require little from you. So during this conversation, look, listen, and smell. Note the data, and when that conversation is over and everyone is seated, begin where it leads you.

BIN 2.

The Client as a Spiritual, Culture-Specific Person

The Family as Spiritual People Belonging to a Specific Culture

WE HAVE JUST PUT great emphasis on observing all the physical aspects about the client and the family. But, of course, there is much more to us humans. Therapists often forget that spirituality and culture provide the underpinnings of a family unit's life. It is within the context of culture and spirituality that everything the therapist says will be interpreted and worked through. And yet, in my experience with trainees, this is usually the bin most lacking in content. It's as if we were not permitted to ask about religion and culture, despite the pride that we Americans have in our cultural diversity and religious tolerance. To make it a little easier, this chapter is broken down into two sections: "Spirituality" and "Culture."

The Spiritual Person

Within the spiritual realm, the therapist should be interested in three aspects in particular: religion, conscience, and values.

1. *Religion*

A number of studies in the literature demonstrate that people with sound religious views and affiliations do better in handling life's stresses than those without such a support system. On the other hand, some clients or their families may perceive strongly held religious views as safeguards against *all* therapeutic interventions and *all* examinations of whatever trauma may have occurred. It is not the therapist's job to judge whether one religion is more valuable or important than another. It is, however, important for the therapist to be reasonably well acquainted with at least most of the world's major religions. For one thing, it will help in finding language that the client can understand. For example, if a client is a devout biblical Christian, it may be helpful to frame the problems the family is having in a biblical context. It could be quite helpful to see how that particular religious belief deals with the problem at hand.

> **Example**: In a very Christian family, Third Way Center client K's mother could not forgive her own mother. She refused to speak to her or even let K see her grandmother, even though the grandmother was a great resource to K and could meet many of her needs (which the mother could not). This was not because Grandmother was in any way directly involved with K's trauma. Mother was merely ashamed of what had happened to K, and feared her own mother's judgmental attitude. By invoking the Fifth Commandment in its entirety, the therapist helped Mother see that reconciliation with her own mother was necessary to K's progress. And Grandmother, too, could deal with her attitude about her daughter's perceived guilt through a more "Christian," forgiving approach.

It may also be possible or even advisable to call on a pastor, priest, rabbi, or imam to help form an alliance with the family and the client. If fundamentalist or ultraconservative religious values are involved, this may be of particular help, though it will likely complicate the alliance process unless the therapist is of the same religious persuasion. If not, then acceptance and close knowledge of the extreme religious views will be necessary to form the beginnings of an alliance. The therapist's understanding of the spiritual and religious views should be complete enough to make the client and the family feel accepted; otherwise, this issue alone can create much difficulty for the client and make trauma therapy impossible.

> **Example:** Client R was struggling with major identity issues, believing he was gay. But he could not tell his fundamentalist parents, or even bring it up, because of their strong antigay religious stance. The therapist initially had to listen so empathically that the parents felt accepted. As that issue was explored further and quotes from the Bible were discussed openly, the discovery was made that there were, in fact, gay members in the parents' families. With this discussion, they softened their stance and R was allowed to explore his own sexuality. He then could turn to the business of trauma recovery.

Religion also often plays a major role in whether the client and family accept therapy and medication. It is equally important to know how well the client or the family adheres to the religious tenets of their particular religious affiliation. The grandmother of one Third Way Center client believed devoutly and fiercely that her granddaughter's abortion was a mortal sin, and so she could not forgive her. But being gently reminded of Christ's saying that he came for the sinners and not the righteous allowed her eventually, like Christ, to forgive and to reconcile with the granddaughter.

Religion can be a great divider or a great unifier in families. It is also something the therapist can ally with if she or he has a strong religious affiliation. On the other hand, it can create great countertransferences in the therapist and the family. If the client is Muslim, for example, the present climate of conflict in the Middle East could easily be a serious obstacle to an alliance. It is also important to know if *no* religion or particular spirituality is present in the client or the family. The whole concept of justice *for* the client (as victim) rather than justice rendered *by* the client might be foreign in the context of some religious beliefs. And indeed, justice has two faces: one for the perpetrator, which demands that restoration be made to the victim (as determined by the justice system), and one for the victim, who needs to see justice done—justice determined by the victim alone. Family members, staff, or people on the larger treatment team may firmly believe that justice is to be meted out by God or the adult world alone. Yet few will believe that wrongdoing should not be punished and that penance should not be done by the perpetrator. To meld these two concepts into a workable whole, by which everyone will permit the client to pursue his or her inner child's need for justice, will take great skill and sensitivity on the part of the primary therapist.

2. Conscience

Whether a client and the family have a good sense of right and wrong will also play a large part in how successful the client is in giving up the problematic behavior and whether they will be able to return to their family and society at large. Most of our clients at Third Way Center are very much connected to the sense of right and wrong that their family adheres to. And it is not necessarily the same sense of right and wrong that a therapist might assume based on the family's religion.

For example, a great many gang-affiliated families attend Christian religious services faithfully. Christianity clearly forbids violent or criminal activity, yet they participate in criminal gang activity anyway. This makes conscience a very fluid and uncertain matter for our clients and will be an important treatment issue. Morality thus becomes a very elusive value, and one that the therapist might seem at times to be pursuing in vain. Morality may then have to be taught again starting with a very early developmental stage—a stage in which the child adheres to right and wrong only because they are told to and because reward and punishment are attached to each behavior. For some of our clients, "good" behavior has little if anything to do with right or wrong. They have been taught, often by the justice system, to comply outwardly no matter what, and comply they do—but only as long as an outside force demands it "or else." Many families have said to our clients, "Just do what they want you to do, say what they want you to say, so you can get out. Fake it to make it." The implication is that once you get out of the system, you can do as you wish, never mind what's right or wrong. The therapist has to make the same determination of whether the family, too, works only on a reward-or-punishment system. Unfortunately, it is sometimes not possible to find the family's stand on this issue until the treatment process is well under way.

The one test on the mental status exam (see Appendix 4) to address this issue with the client is the judgment questions, which will greatly help the therapist determine how much of a conscience the client has. This part of the evaluation also will foreshadow the issues of box 4: the issues of justice for the client, and the family's help or opposition to resolving them. If, for example, the offender is part of the family, how willing will the offender be to atone for the injustice done to the client or the family? Often, the family is unwilling to give up the offender, for fear that they will lose the physical or financial support that the offender provides.

Example: X had reported her abuse, and her father was to go to trial on charges of sexual abuse. When the prosecuting attorneys subpoenaed her, she refused to comply. Her mother had pleaded with her because the mother was unemployed and the father was the only person who could support the severely handicapped older sister. She did not deny that what he had done was wrong, only that justice should not be done at this time. It took a lot of work to find solutions to the issue of the sister, such as getting a great-aunt to come forward as support, before X decided that she could now testify. Of course, the mother first had to approve the solution that X and her therapist had found regarding who would care for the sister. Only then would the mother give her sanction—reluctantly—for X to testify.

The therapist will often be put in these difficult situations, weighing right and wrong. At the outset of this process of healing, our clients are usually already thoroughly convinced that there is no justice and that only children have to atone, never adults. It is therefore important to note what the family's attitude is toward atonement versus vengeance; versus believing that God forgives anyway, that one can never get justice, or that justice can be gotten only when it is convenient.

3. Values

All families value certain traits more than others in their members. Whether our adolescent clients fit those family values is significant and important. Some families value aggressiveness and self-reliance—even what the law would deem excessive aggressiveness. Other families value reliance on family and culture as the family perceives it. Client and family may have no spirituality and value only material things.

When the therapist is first taking a history from the client and the family, values are often difficult to discern since this is a subject not easily discussed. True family values may not emerge until sometime during the course of treatment, and then only through the therapist's recognition of the judgmental statements that the client or the family makes. This is probably one of the most common points where, on an unconscious level, the therapist may encounter strong countertransference issues, since most therapists and treatment staff at Third Way Center come from very different value systems compared to those of their clients and families. This makes for misunderstandings, and they happen easily. Countertransference issues around differing value systems, especially by the larger treatment team members such as caseworker or client managers, rarely facilitate—and may deeply impede— the treatment process.

For example, a therapist or caseworker may feel appalled by a client's family values around cleanliness, blame the mother for the perceived lack of hygiene, and dislike the mother of the client, thus hindering a reconciliation with the client even though this may be what the client needs and wants. Sometimes, the value issue is surprising and unexpected.

> **Example:** An entire therapy and social service system wrote B off as being deeply disturbed and unable to function in several previous treatment centers. She did indeed speak as if she were much more intelligent than she was, even though what she said was often nonsense. Upon taking a careful family-values history, the Third Way Center therapist discovered that everyone within that family system had a doctorate and worked at highly skilled technical jobs. The entire family and the social service system were very proud and deeply

invested in the achievements of this intelligent, likable family. But B had many learning deficits, and her IQ, though within low-normal limits, was way below her family's. She was trying desperately to keep up with what the family valued most, and was deeply ashamed of her deficits, which became more and more obvious as she progressed in school. Much of her acting out was in the attempt to hide this. Her trauma was that she did not fit into this family, and the family had to broaden its acceptance of other valuable human traits besides high intelligence.

Culture

The United States is famous for being a cultural melting pot, and most of us are quite proud of this without really knowing much about it. That's because, with so many cultures living side by side in the United States, it is hard to learn even their most basic predominant features. Never mind learning what the "relevant" features might be! This bewildering cultural diversity also makes the therapist's job difficult. What may be abnormal in one culture may be perfectly acceptable in another. And to give the pot an added stir, no two families within a culture interpret that same culture identically.

> **Example:** When V came to Third Way Center, the referring agency told the staff that she hallucinated and was therefore diagnosed with a psychotic illness. She came from a deeply religious Filipino family, and her mother had died within that year. She often spoke of having both "seen" and "talked to" her mother. Within her religious and cultural background, this was considered normal and most certainly did not suggest a psychotic

process. She did, however, suffer a traumatic grief reaction. This does not mean that *all* Filipinos, even deeply religious ones, mourn in this way, but within her particular subculture, this way of grieving was well accepted.

Culture, along with religious beliefs, is often a contributor to our value system. Religious beliefs are sometimes strongly linked to culture, as the above case illustrates. But a word of caution is in order. Even within a culture, great differences exist between individuals. That is, not *all* Germans, Mexicans, or Vietnamese are alike. The therapist may think so, but most often this is just the therapist's own prejudice leading to countertransference. Not all immigrants are the same, nor all African Americans. Not all women are alike (despite what some men may think), just as not all men are alike. There are vast differences between members of a culture or ethnic group. David Cannadine's recently published book *The Undivided Past* makes the point that it is actually quite difficult to divide humankind into distinct races, let alone into distinct cultures or socioeconomic groups.

Still, major differences often do exist, certainly in language. At Third Way Center, we also see a great many foreign-born children who have been adopted from another country or whose parents have recently immigrated. These children have managed, more or less successfully, to integrate into the mainstream U.S. culture, though this has often taken a great toll on them and their families. The adopting family's inability to see or understand the cultural differences between themselves and their adopted child has often resulted in deeply disturbed family relationships despite the best intentions of both parties. Children in immigrant families often suffer in similar ways because it is their parents who cannot see or understand the mainstream American culture.

Example: L was adopted from Bulgaria by a well-meaning Longmont couple who did not speak or learn a single word of Bulgarian before or after the adoption. L was 7 at the time and spoke no English. By the time adolescence had set in, L was angry and acting out. In sociological terms, she was a "marginal man"—a person between two cultures and belonging to neither. No wonder she felt unconnected and dispossessed! Not belonging culturally is a major trauma, but the attempt to integrate into a new culture can lead to post-traumatic stress disorder, particularly if the dominant culture is hostile to that integration. And on top of this, add the trauma resulting from the adopted child's inability to understand a single person in her new American environment.

Then there are all the multifarious subcultures in U.S. society, especially among adolescents. Of those subcultures, the one most often affecting the course of therapy is the gang lifestyle. For many adolescents, it offers protection and vindication for environmental trauma, and yet, it makes getting to that trauma and resolving it nearly impossible. Another problem is that so many entire families are involved in the gang lifestyle, often generationally, making the resistance to therapy seemingly insurmountable because of the secrecy and resistance to change within that subculture.

Another subculture is the world of lesbian, gay, bisexual, and transgender adolescents—and, often, their parents—who face an entirely different cultural problem. Though often more open to treatment than other subcultures, they may meet more countertransference on the part of their treatment team.

There are, of course, innumerable other cultural subgroups that have great significance to teens. These can wax or wane in popularity over the years. One example is the Deadhead culture that lasted for decades around the band the Grateful Dead. In a later generation, the hip-hop group Insane Clown Posse has its own following. It is therefore vitally important for adolescent therapists to be reasonably well acquainted with popular cultural trends.

Culture deeply influences much of the therapeutic process: the alliances to be made, responses to medication issues, degree of trust in helping personnel, value systems. It certainly influences the approach the therapist must take, even in the initial interview. It most of all influences the choice of words, the complexity of sentences, and the concepts the therapist should use in the process of history taking and alliance formation. It might be necessary at times to get an interpreter, not just for language differences, but also for cultural interpretations. Or it may be more useful to communicate directly, nonverbally, with a foreign-language-speaking client, through drawings, gestures, or play.

It is certainly helpful for all therapists—for everyone on the treatment team—to be acutely aware of what prejudices around cultural issues may come up in treatment personnel as well as in the client and family. Everyone has prejudices, though these may be more or less under control. Every therapist likes to think him- or herself free from all prejudice, because, as one caseworker pointed out to me, therapists are "trained not to be prejudiced." It follows, then, that all therapists should be free of countertransference. What high moral ground might we then be able to reach as therapists! But we can manage prejudices only if we are acutely aware of them. Once aware of the bias, we can look around and find a mentor or supervisor who is more knowledgeable, more culturally or spiritually competent in this area of the history-taking process, and ask for help.

BIN 3.

The Client as Psychological Person

Each Family member as a Psychological Person

EVERY PERSON, even an adolescent, has an "inner" life, a way of making sense of what happens on the outside, in the world of reality. The inner life includes everything that originates inside the person: feelings, images, random thoughts, dreams. The two worlds, the inner and the outer, have to be more or less reconciled. Therapy is very much affected by the way this happens or does not happen for the client and the family. Everyone struggles with finding pathways by which they try to make sense of their total world. This is the interplay between what they perceive to be the outer reality, and the needs of the inner world of feelings and thoughts.

In the history-taking process, three areas are of particular interest to the therapist:

- What did psychological testing show?
- What are the client's and the family's IQs?

- What are the client's and the family's ego functions?
- concept formation (especially since the idea of justice is a concept)
- defense mechanisms
- reality testing

1. Psychological Testing and Mental Status Exam

Much of a person's psychological makeup can be found in previous psych testing in the chart and through a full mental status exam (see Appendix 4). The mental status exam should always be administered by the primary therapist, who will be with the client throughout the entire history-gathering and treatment process. The mental status exam gives the following information that is pertinent to evaluating the client's psychological functions:

- possibility of an organic problem (orientation, figure drawings)
- intelligence (fund of knowledge)
- working memory (objects to remember and memory questions)
- reality testing (proverbs and similarities)
- anxiety levels (numbers forward and backward and subtractions)

It is seldom possible to administer the mental status exam to all relevant family members; thus, the other information in this section will have to be acquired through observation during the history-taking process. For example, do the stories make sense? Can the therapist follow the history as given by the family member? How closely do the various histories obtained from different family members match?

2. IQ

It is crucial that the therapist have some idea of the IQ of the client and the family, along with any learning deficits that might affect that IQ. If a cognitive assessment exists, as it does for most Department of Youth Corrections clients, this is very helpful because of its emphasis on verbal comprehension and perceptual reasoning. At the very least, a Woodcock-Johnson test is available to us through Third Way Center's educational department. This gives a relatively clear picture of the client's educational level. Together with an assessment of the family's educational level, the cognitive assessment will inform the therapist on how to use language in a way that the client and the family can understand. And it may even provide a clue to the problem within the family. For example, in a family where everyone has advanced college degrees, a child's perfectly adequate IQ of 100 or 95 could be treated as a terrible, shameful handicap.

Also, if the family or the teen has severe auditory or language handicaps, talking to them will be difficult. The therapist will have to find alternative ways of communicating. It is no good talking to someone who does not speak or understand English or does not understand the spoken words (because of an auditory perceptual handicap, for example). Therapists are, of course, almost exclusively trained in talking and talking and talking, in a somewhat complicated and decidedly middle-class manner. But little time in their training goes toward learning to communicate visually or in simple, concrete ways. It may be necessary to communicate only through drawings or journals. It may even be necessary to use some form of sign language or a combination of communication styles.

> **Example:** D had been admitted to Third Way Center after over twenty failed placements in which he was found to be severely handicapped by PTSD symptoms.

He was also often combative and terribly uncooperative. It quickly became apparent through some basic
testing that he had a profoundly incapacitating auditory processing handicap, which left him understanding less than 10 percent of what was being said to him,
especially when he was anxious or angry. Whenever
he became angry or anxious, he could hear only the
tone of what was being said, without understanding the
words, and it frightened him, so he lashed out. He was
much like the *Peanuts* comic-strip character Charlie
Brown, who heard all adults saying only "Blah, blah,
blah." Despite its having been noted two years before
he came to Third Way Center, therapists at all placements—including Third Way Center staff initially—
continued to talk and talk to D. And, of course, they
did all the orientation through talking. To everyone's
surprise, he got none of the rules! Staff had to learn
simple sign language and to communicate in written
form. D, for his part, eventually had to learn, instead
of becoming combative, to tell others around him that
he did not understand what was being said. He had to
let others know that although he was not deaf, he could
not understand the words, so shouting at him wouldn't
help. Only once we found a way to communicate with
him could we begin to address his trauma.

Words that seem simple to a therapist and are commonly used
may be totally foreign to the client and the family. How complicated or
uncomplicated their vocabulary is, for example, may give clues about
their IQ. In the course of history taking, this has to be noted. It's helpful to ask the client and the family at times to repeat what they heard

the therapist say, or to ask them whether they think the therapist has gotten the history correctly. During this interchange, note the difficulties encountered.

3. Ego Functions

a) Concept Formation

As noted earlier, we can get an idea of the client's concept formation ability through the mental status exam, by administering the proverb and similarities tests. Essentially, this means that the therapist needs to know whether the client and the family can make a correct category of what appear to be disparate ideas. For example, making up for past misdeeds may involve apologizing, doing community service, being incarcerated, and so on, but still, all of this amounts to doing penance and involves justice—a *concept*. For some of Third Way Center's clients, life is an endless series of Groundhog Days in which the same events repeat endlessly without the client's perceiving any connection. Similarly, even painful events never seem to form a category; that is, every time this event occurs, pain and suffering follow. Even being able to see that whenever the client does A, B then follows might be a step toward the process of concept formation. Sometimes, this inability is not so much lack of intelligence or inability to form concepts as it is the fear of a *specific* concept, a concept to be avoided at all costs—such as sexual abuse trauma.

> **Example:** L had been at Third Way Center for quite some time, and although she had made sufficient behavioral progress to move into ever less restrictive settings, she kept picking up boyfriends who were invariably abusive and harmful to her. They were clearly (or so it appeared to all staff) basically the same kind of person and remarkably like her abuser. And

yet, she seemed unable to see that all her boyfriends' actions, though different in their particulars, fit the category of abuse.

b) Defense Mechanisms

Every family and every client has a preferred way to defend against anxiety and unpleasant psychological issues. So do therapists, for that matter, and this can interfere as often as the client's own defense mechanisms. Much of the choice and style of defense mechanism depends on IQ, education, and family tradition. A more complex and, perhaps, more valued defense mechanism, such as sublimation, is just as difficult to deal with as a more primitive one, such as denial. But sublimation might also be connected with altruism and, therefore, be easier to weave into the treatment process. Sublimation is often employed by deeply religious people who have given their idea of what justice might be up to God and have turned their sad and angry feelings over to religion or AA. If no symptoms are apparent and the victim is functioning well, then sublimation works well and is perfectly acceptable—and fortunate—for that person.

But most of our clients have underlying biological structural defects that have made sublimation or any other higher defense mechanisms impossible to practice. On the other hand, plain denial, employed as a defense mechanism by the client and the family, will take a lot of explaining, in language and a manner appropriate to IQ and concept formation, about why it is detrimental to the client and the family. Because denial is one of the most primitive forms of all defense mechanisms and is much beloved by adolescents, it requires a relatively unsophisticated approach of endless persistence and a great deal of humor.

> **Example:** I encountered L on the back porch of a Third
> Way Center residential treatment facility when I drove
> up. He was smoking. I knew that he was on a smoking
> restriction and actually grounded. When I approached
> him, he no longer seemed to be smoking and denied
> that he had been. But smoke was coming from his
> right pant pocket, and I suggested he put it out before
> his pants caught fire. It was both sad and funny, and
> certainly childlike, that he would deny his trouble-
> some behavior even though he still got consequences for
> breaking the rules.

If denial is the most commonly used defense mechanism in the teens, projection is probably the second most common, especially in teens who have been in correctional facilities. It is always someone else's fault that the teen got into trouble and acted out. Of course, this is also often the preferred defense mechanism of their families, too. Since "others" are indeed quite annoying, provocative, and in endless supply and since poverty and discrimination add a great deal of pressure and veracity to this belief, dealing with this particularly vexing defensive system may take some time. Considering that most treatment at Third Way Center takes place in the milieu, peer feedback and in-the-moment clarification are instrumental in getting the client to see this defense mechanism and its uselessness. Forming strong alliances with the client and the family decreases the need for this defense mechanism.

Since defensive systems come into play when anxiety levels are high, it's important to see that when defenses are up, it is generally because anxiety is up. Therefore, lowering the client's and the family's anxiety level might decrease the need for the defense mechanism. It is also sometimes helpful to deal with defense mechanisms directly. A particular defense mechanism may add to countertransference issues emerging in the therapist, because most therapists have difficulty tolerating our clients' or their families' projection of all their problems onto the therapist. It is also these defense mechanisms that may make atonement and restorative justice hard to achieve, because they make empathy on the part of the therapist very difficult. Thus, the therapist has difficulty seeing the need for justice for the misbehaving client. A family or a client who persistently blames the therapist for all the difficulties they encounter is not easy to be empathic with. It will take team support for the therapist to see the desperation of that client and the family. And only then does empathy on the part of the therapist become possible. When the client or the family becomes defensive and anxious, it is a clue to the therapist that the therapist must change course or alleviate some impediment in the milieu.

c) Reality Testing

Whatever stands between what the client feels and what the world outside presents is mediated by the person's ego, or sense of self. It is that ego that makes reality testing—knowing what reality is—possible. People with a lot of trauma or with devastating trauma feel tremendous internal emotional pressure, which colors all perception and, therefore, all reality. The ability to keep those two forces apart and evaluate them and then integrate them is often severely compromised in our clients and their families. While listening to the history, it is important, especially in family interactions, to listen carefully and note whether the information that the family presents makes sense and is logical. For example, clients and (especially) families often make mutually contradictory statements. When this is pointed out, some families will look puzzled and refuse to accept that the statements are contradictory, while others will correct themselves and explain the incongruent statements more or less in a way that the therapist can understand.

Before we can proceed to treatment, reality testing must be intact, or the causes for the impaired reality testing must be determined. For example, is the problem anxiety provoked? Or is it intrinsic and structural, as with schizophrenia or affective dysregulation with psychosis? In those cases, psychopharmacology may be necessary before the treatment process can begin. Correcting the underlying faulty reality testing will be necessary for both the client and the family.

> **Example:** When C was admitted to Third Way Center, he had run from many other placements and was spending most of his time on the streets and living under bridges with other homeless people. He explained that he felt most comfortable with them, that they "understood" him. Talking to him, it quickly became apparent that he suffered from schizophrenia, and formal psychological testing confirmed this diagnosis. It took time to get him to accept his diagnosis and agree to medications. It took more time to get him on the right antipsychotics, but then he stopped running away and functioned well. Only after he was adequately medicated was it finally time to look at his history, which was riddled with abuse and abandonment. Only with his underlying structural genetic defect under control was it possible to deal with his trauma, which was indeed considerable. But in the end, he was able to deal with this, and even the death of his mother did not keep him from getting healthy.

It takes all of a client's strength and thinking ability to manage the process of healing the trauma. And even then there may be situations in which the client's illness itself represents the trauma. And if the client refuses to accept that the illness represents trauma, it becomes difficult indeed to overcome. In any case, few adolescents can easily accept that they are not "perfect" or that they may have been born with a major handicap.

> **Example:** F was born with a condition of atrophied legs, which had to be amputated shortly after birth. All through his childhood, he had handled it "well" and even learned to play basketball, becoming quite a virtuoso with his wheelchair. But in adolescence, he became defiant, reckless, and angry. It turned out that he blamed his mother for her decision to have his legs amputated, and that neither he nor his mother could accept that he was less than perfect. All his life, he had been raised to be a self-centered child by a guilt-ridden mother who could never say no to him. The whole world seemed to revolve around him. His narcissism so severely impaired his reality testing that he refused to wear his prostheses. He continued to walk on his stumps, even running races on them, to the point of serious injury. Both he and his family maintained that he was quite "perfect" and that nobody was troubled by his situation. Thus, his rage and resentment were quickly covered and denied, so he could never get in touch with those feelings long enough to do therapy. Neither his family nor he was willing to accept that this unrealistic point of view was harming him.

Although this attempt to see how the psychological processes work within the client and the family members is essential, it is by no means a complete psychological evaluation of either client or family.

Nor does it make formal, specific psychological or neuropsychological testing unnecessary. This protocol will, however, point out areas where further psychological information, obtained through formal testing, may be not only helpful but necessary.

BIN 4.

The Client as a Member of a Member of a Family, Nuclear as well as Extended

The Nuclear Family as Part of an Extended Family

FAMILIES ARE THE SINGLE most important factor in understanding a client, and the single most influential agent in trauma recovery. As the saying goes, mothers always win! And they tend to be the center of most families. Many examples given in the previous chapters focus on what the mother of the client thought, permitted, and wanted. Typically, it is not cost effective for the therapist to go against nature, since the bond between mother and child—even when weakened by severe neglect and abandonment—remains, by nature, a determining factor in the child's life. It is well worth keeping this rule in mind always when evaluating a family.

Another saying worth remembering is that blood is thicker than water. Therefore, it is never helpful to align oneself against a family, no matter how dysfunctional it may appear. The overt anger and rage that many of our clients exhibit is often directed not against the abuser but against the mother, who is seen either as not having protected our client or as not believing that the abuse, the injury, occurred. Despite this, the wish to be reconciled and have the mother change remains fundamental in each client. Once a child is bonded to the mother, the bond remains basically unbroken, whether the mother is good, bad, or indifferent. That makes the influence the mother has over the client instrumental in the client's recovery. One of the maxims I have learned over the years is that no matter how much the client or the family rages against the mother, because of that biologically determined bond, the mother does always win. For practical purposes, it is important to learn that. Many a therapist has been caught up in that conflict, to the point that they completely forget the origin of any and all trauma. Families themselves become deeply divided and blame the mother in the same manner as the client, making nonjudgmental, empathic neutrality even harder.

That said, this section of the history-taking process concerns itself with families and how they work or don't work. This section has to be addressed within the very first week, preferably on the day the client arrives at Third Way Center. As already noted, most families have been in the social service system, or dealing with therapists, for some time. And very few, if any, of them are happy with the results. They won't likely be glad to hear from yet another therapist or be eager to cooperate. Most will give the therapist only about five seconds to say something interesting enough to make them want to continue a conversation, let alone cooperate with the history-taking process. It is best not to use traditional opening phrases learned in graduate school—they already know them by heart. Acquainting oneself with the previous history and taking advice from the client may be much more helpful and provide ideas and phrases to approach the family with. Sounding reasonably informed about the case may help establish an alliance and shows respect to the family.

Example: R's mother had had innumerable confrontations with her son's caseworker. When she came through the front door of the facility, she was angry, strutting, and rude to staff. I also knew from R that his mother thought all therapists were useless and "wimps." When she arrived, I happened to be in the hall and immediately pointed out to her that this was my house and being rude would not fly. We instantly got into an argument. I stayed with it, and standing up to her made it possible for her to air her grievances and eventually share her great worries around her son. I had decided to "speak her language" and was not afraid to argue with her or to listen to what she had to say. I had gotten her attention. Without that, it is very hard to get real information from either the client or the family.

Bin 4, the category for evaluating families, has two divisions: (1) the *genogram* and (2) the *family function.* Family function is further broken down into the nuclear family and the extended family (which must include both the maternal and the paternal side).

1. Genogram

The genogram will provide clues to who might be able to help in the therapeutic process. This, after all, is one of the clues that answer the important question: who can be most helpful in the healing process of the six boxes? If many family members are functioning well, the process will be vastly easier. The more healthy support there is within the family, the easier it will be to get some form of justice from an abuser and to enlist the family's help in this quest.

At Third Way Center, we have very few clients with a traditional two-biological-parent family. The concept of family, with our clients and in society as a whole, has expanded. It includes adoptive families in which the client may or may not know one or the other biological parent, kinship "parents" such as grandparents or other relatives raising the client, one biological parent and a stepparent, with the other biological parent involved or uninvolved, no parents and multiple foster parents, an interested foster parent, a single parent who has lost contact or wants no contact with the other parent, a single adoptive parent, and so on. Even within these categories, we find more variations.

The genogram must include all this and, along with it, the extended families of all family members involved, as much as is possible. This is often so difficult to do that the temptation is either just to accept what is noted in the intake or the previous records, or just to forget it and concentrate solely on the client. The inclusion of the extended family will yield information on family patterns, such as patterns of relationships, patterns of success or failure, and patterns of functioning. The more people are known who are, were, or might be in the client's life, the more likely that both abusers and great supporters will be discovered. So this information will affect both the trauma and the cure, though gathering it nearly always represents a difficult and time-consuming effort by the therapist. But it places people within the client's life in time and space, and it will be useful to refer to in writing, during therapy, since most of our clients have incredibly confusing and complicated family patterns.

Another source of material for the genogram, as well as for family function (discussed below), is the mental status exam. (See Appendix 4.) With the mental status exam comes the task of drawing a family portrait. Mother Nature made adolescents lazy, so they will most often try to draw stick figures. Not acceptable. With encouragement—perhaps strong insistence—they will typically draw a more or less adequate picture of their nuclear family. Much about the alliances within that family can be seen in that picture. The picture is noteworthy not only for who it shows in what position, but also for who is absent from the picture or for how unrealistic and filled with wishful thinking it is. It is vitally important to discuss the family portrait extensively with the client. It matters who the client considers to be the nuclear family, whether adopted or biological. For some of our clients, there is no nuclear family at the time of admission, making the mental status task even more telling about what the client might perceive to be the nuclear family. It is not always easy, during the client's short stay at Third Way Center, to locate all significant family members. Parents often have lost custody or have had their rights terminated. It is at this juncture that the needs of the court system and the needs of the client most often clash. Outside agencies may put up considerable resistance to letting the therapist evaluate significant family members. It is important to stress to the client, the involved family members, and the treatment team that the goal at this point is most certainly *not* reunification but, rather, to evaluate the significant family members' functioning and usefulness in the therapeutic process. Most families are afraid that the new information that might— and, indeed, very often does—emerge will contradict their perception, or that long-held and cherished family secrets might be revealed. Or they fear that secrets long kept and rationalized as insignificant could surface and that therapists might find them "significant." Nonetheless, it is important therapeutically that the therapist get to see the patterns of functioning within the whole family system, and how the client may have learned to function. Though the chart usually contains much information that seems judgmental, most often this is merely information passed from one agency to another—and, like the telephone game that children play, badly distorted by the time the client arrives at Third Way Center.

2. Family Function

After the genogram is done, it is important to determine how well or how poorly the family members function and how they interact (or avoid interacting) with each other.

The Nuclear Family

This unit consists of the biological father, biological mother, and biological siblings. Most of our clients, as noted, may not have the traditional nuclear family or they may be able to recall only a few family members or caretaking foster families, but those few are significant and should be included because they, too, have deeply influenced the client by how well or how poorly they functioned. When looking at who in the family might be important, it is worth asking the client and the family *who* the client most resembles, and *whose* life they might be duplicating by the script the family has written for the client. Every family—even a foster family—assigns its members certain roles and functions. This is often based on physical or behavioral similarities between members. Or it may be based on some similarity in their histories. On this basis, our client's family—whether the biological family, adoptive family, or foster family, has its notions of what and who our client is like The same is true, of course, for the people within the social welfare system: they, too, assign roles to their clients and the clients' families.

Though most of this scripting is negative, it is also vitally important in determining who in the family is successful and might be available as a role model for the client and as an ally to the therapist. For example, if the entire family appears gang involved, whether with the same or with rival gangs, it is important to find at least one family member who has escaped this script, or else it will be difficult, if not impossible, for the client not to be gang involved.

In divorce cases, it is *crucial* to hear both sides impartially. As the history is taken, it may become obvious that the previous therapists and caseworkers have aligned themselves with one or the other parent in the divorce. It is generally the side that is most outwardly cooperative and accessible, thereby giving the history of how the family functions a very one-sided, skewed appearance. Therefore, extreme efforts have to be made to get both parents' input—even more so when a grandparent on the maternal or paternal side has been the acting parent of our client. Chances are, there will be much resistance to this process, and it is important to make the protesting party comfortable with the idea that gathering information is not the same as taking sides. We are not trying to reunify the client with the other parent, or even sharing information. The resistance needs to be addressed, and fears allayed, first. Despite the difficulties, the process of getting both sides of the history is crucial.

> **Example:** When K came to Third Way Center, he had been in over 17 placements, had refused to get adopted, and had lost all contact with the family. He looked as though he was always waiting for his family to come back. Because the family had lost custody and all contact, the caseworker was understandably reluctant to give the therapist permission to try to find the biological family. After much discussion of the purpose of the search for the biological family, and after establishing parameters for the contact, the caseworker gave permission. When the biological grandparents were found, not only were they helpful sources of information, but they had exhausted their financial resources trying to find K. He had been waiting for them as eagerly as they were looking for him, and though he did not go and live with them, they remained a great support for him and gave him a long-sought sense of belonging to *some-*

one. It is good to remember that he had this longing in common with most of our clients, who all need and want to belong to someone.

The Extended Family

This includes uncles, aunts, grandparents, cousins, and as many relatives—adopted as well as foster—as can or will get involved in the client's life. Often, this is so time consuming that the therapist forgets about it, but if it is always an open question for the therapist and has been included in the genogram, the therapist will continue to gather information on the extended family and its functioning throughout the entire process of therapy. Some families have included in the concept of "extended family" neighbors, close friends, gang affiliates, church members, and so on. It is often through contact with this entire "extended family" that we discover the traumas that our clients have suffered. It is also often in that "extended family" that we find someone who can and will step forward to help our client heal. As in K's example above, it was the grandparents who not only knew where other family members were who also needed and wanted contact, but also could shed light on the traumas that K had suffered as a child. They, with verification by other family members, were able to provide for K and his therapist a *history*—a sense of continuity and understanding of why and how his troubles had started—and to provide options for how to heal the traumas of his childhood. It is often in the extended family, as in the gang-involved family mentioned earlier, that we find a cousin, second cousin, or *someone* who has been able to avoid gang membership. It is often the extended-family member with the least to lose who can paint the clearest picture of what happened to our client.

Example: In the earlier example of X, who had been adopted from Bulgaria at age 7, it was noted that she did not speak English, and her adoptive family did not speak a word of Bulgarian. Nonetheless, she was told how unhappy the childhood was that her adoptive parents had supposedly rescued her from. They wanted her to have no contact with her biological mother. But X had found her Bulgarian biological mother, who was working in Germany at the time. They could not really communicate, because of the language barrier. The more anxious X became, the more she acted out until, with permission from her adoptive parents, her therapist procured a translator. A dialogue with the biological mother ensued. The biological mother told X how she had lost her even though she wanted to keep her, and thus began a long process of healing. This process was able to start even after X learned that her mother had not quite told the truth. But closure was still both possible and necessary. For it is finding the truth, no matter how painful, that makes the healing process possible. In fact, through that process of finding her mother, she also found siblings who wanted to have a close relationship with her.

In the treatment of children and adolescents, families have always been, and will continue to be, a vexing and difficult problem. Even really run-of-the-mill adolescents have deeply unresolved feelings about their families. They both love and hate the family, want them to know they suffer, and want them to stay out of their business, all at the same time. Being sensitive to that, remembering one's own adolescence without letting it interfere, makes navigating family therapy easier.

BIN 5.

The Client as a Socioeconomic Person

The Family as a Socioeconomic Unit

1. The Social Person

We, all of us, are social persons. This includes the client and the client's family. They have friends. They socialize. They engage in sexual activity—sometimes appropriately, sometimes not. And they impose or receive discipline.

a) Friends

It seems obvious that all clients and their family members have friends and socialize. It is also obvious that more of those friends are likely to be gang members than debutantes and honorees on the society pages. We think of ourselves as too sophisticated to fall for clichés and stereotypes, and yet, without thinking twice, we expect "birds of a feather" to "flock together." Like all clichés, this one bore true often enough to stick. But to assume that it is *always* true would be a mistake. Thus, we cannot presume to know someone else's social circle. Knowing requires asking, exploring the subject. Is the family especially isolated, or do they have a wide circle of friends? How well do they get along with their friends? It is often helpful to invite families to bring a friend to the interview, especially if that friend happens to be, say, a member of the clergy. Clergy can be extremely good at helping families face their difficulties, and it is often easier for families to take advice, and even what they perceive as criticism, if it comes from a trusted family friend or clergy member. Most therapists don't make enough use of the client's or the family's friends. More often, they are forced by the adolescents themselves to meet their friends. Confidentiality rules have made this avenue of inquiry more complicated, but it isn't really that difficult to get a client or family to invite friends to meetings with the therapist after clear parameters are set around what can and what cannot be discussed.

Clients and families behave differently with friends than with therapists or people they perceive as being associated with the social service system. Too often, clients have completely separate and parallel lives that can undo in an hour what took the therapist a month to accomplish. This is true even in a residential setting such as Third Way Center, though there are innumerable opportunities in the milieu to unobtrusively observe the client interacting with peers. Most adolescent clients are terribly reluctant to share their therapist with their friends, or vice versa. Most of their real friends don't even know that they are in placement, let alone that the client is a "client"—that is, that he or she is in need of "therapy." A teen's friend has to be invited in by the therapist, and this invitation will nearly always meet with resistance. When the client allows a friend to join a session, it's usually a sign that the therapist has made a strong, positive alliance with the client. Also, few families tell their friends that their child is in placement. This makes eliciting information on family friends difficult.

b) *Socializing*

Recognizing that all humans are social beings also means that the therapist should ask about what the family does for entertainment. It matters whether they prefer to do drugs or play bridge. It matters whether they find entertainment individually or as a family unit, and how much of the family's resources go toward entertainment. Do they go hiking together? Watch football or baseball or basketball together? Do they actually play on a team? Being a team member requires an ability to cooperate, and that is a significant helpful attribute in the process of therapy. Partying probably is the most difficult thing to ask about in this section, but it tells a great deal about the family. It is certainly one of the activities that could make a client unsafe. This means, of course, asking about the drug and alcohol use and abuse. Most Third Way Center clients have issues with drugs and alcohol, and so do most of their families. Then there is the whole related issue of drug and alcohol use by both the father and the mother during conception and pregnancy, for it can contribute greatly to the mental illness that may be observable in the client. Or the client's own drug or alcohol use may have caused the mental illness. It is also noteworthy how much danger the clients expose themselves to during what they perceive to be "party time." Do rules hold during party time, or do they go out the window?

c) *Sex*

Dating is also part of socializing. Does the client have a girlfriend or boyfriend? And is that person socially and age appropriate as well as helpful to the client? Most difficult of all to ask are the questions about sex. Who is having sex with whom, and how often? Does the client use protection? Then there is the issue of modesty and boundaries, bathroom etiquette, and sleeping arrangements, especially where sexual abuse is suspected. For example, consistently seeing or hearing sexual activity by adults during childhood will appear to most children as

sexual abuse or auditory sexual abuse. Similarly, being exposed to por-
nography appears as sexual abuse. Typically, when the client arrives at
Third Way Center, neither the client nor the abuser sees such exposure
as abuse.

> **Example:** many families videotape their holidays. So
> when client N mentioned that the family had made a
> video when he was home on a Christmas pass, his ther-
> apist asked whether the family would share the tape.
> They agreed. What the many hours of video showed
> was a family slowly becoming disabled by massive
> alcohol intoxication, and N becoming more and more
> isolated as the family grew more and more sexually dis-
> inhibited. The family didn't think they had a problem
> with alcohol or with sex.

Many of the symptoms of sexual abuse in the client are social
impairments, such as chronic lying in girls, and promiscuity and
incessant fighting in boys. How open are family members about sexual
activity? How observable is it to their children? Is there a known sexual
perpetrator in the extended family? Which members of the family have
been sexually abused?

d) Discipline
Discipline is often associated with physical or verbal abuse. What constitutes discipline within the family? Is there physical or verbal abuse?
How do people speak to each other, especially during conflict? Some of
this material, even when asked specifically, might emerge only after an
alliance has been built. And even then it is always surprising how little
a therapist really knows about how the family functions. But to a keen
eye and ear, much of this is observable during the family meetings. It

should be noted how families discipline either the client or the younger siblings. It might be interesting to observe how the siblings discipline each other or deal with conflict. This can give clues to how discipline is handled when a therapist or observer is not present, since most people tend to behave better rather than worse during interview or therapy sessions. Not just words matter. Looks, eye rolling, sighs, and body language should be noted for clues. How respectful are family members to each other? Do they tolerate differences of opinion? Sometimes only one member of the family is allowed to speak, and if others try or are invited by the therapist to speak, they are censored. Of course, this means inviting the entire family—not only the parents (or, even worse, just one parent)—to the family sessions. This despite the fact that during therapy, it may become necessary to see one or the other parent, or a sibling, alone for several sessions.

> **Example:** when V was sent to Third Way Center, it was because he had attacked his mother with a screwdriver and tried to stab her in the back after she refused his request to cook pork chops. When family meetings first began, the family professed to have no idea what the attack was about. Father did all the talking, to the point that a meeting had to be set up with Mother alone. She was frightened and terribly anxious. Not long after that, it became apparent that Father kept the family under his exclusive control by being physically abusive and threatening death and destruction to any family member who rebelled. V was merely acting out Father's response to disagreement. He was acting out, in fact, the very violence that Father threatened to inflict when someone disobeyed.

Example: I had been seeing A with her parents for almost a year. She had all the socially impairing symptoms of having been sexually abused, though it seemed impossible to find out who and where the abuser might be. One day during a session, the mother mentioned in passing that this was the day that A's uncle was getting out of prison. This uncle had never been mentioned before. When asked why he had been in prison, the mother said because he had sexually abused his own and other children. It was not difficult to find A's abuser after that. This clearly demonstrates how difficult it can be to ask just the right questions.

2. Economics

Sadly, therapists are rarely trained to be interested in the economic realities of a client or a family. And yet, money matters. In fact, it matters a great deal. Income, occupation, and housing are key preoccupations of clients and families and have shaped their lives—and, often, their trauma. So no matter how prepared or unprepared the therapist is, these issues must be addressed.

b) Income and Occupation

The amount of income/money and how it is spent within the family system is one of the unspoken taboos in American life and, hence, difficult to ask about. But it matters whether the family has disposable income or barely enough to meet its needs. Income affects everything, even transportation to and from family meetings with the therapist. Income affects the degree of follow-up for the client, and payments for medication. Occupation and income often determine the expectations that the client and the family may have of the therapist, and the prejudices they may harbor against the therapist.

For example, families who have been in the welfare system and jobless tend to have a great deal of resentment and often feel trapped and more helpless than families with an independent income. It also matters where that money is coming from. Though we see few trust fund parents at Third Way Center, their approach to therapy will differ dramatically from that of the family or the client who makes a living by selling or manufacturing drugs, or a family involved in other illicit activities.

How the money is spent is as significant as where it comes from and how much it is. It should be noted, for example, if a family with no discernible income can take a trip to Canada, say, or wear Prada shoes. It also matters how many pets the family supports. Usually, the client is a good source of this information. It may even influence the approach the therapist takes to meet with the family or the way the therapist dresses. For example, when meeting with a particular family, would casual dress be more appropriate than the usual "professional" attire that most therapists have been taught to wear?

> **Example:** G's family had been involved with the social welfare system for at least two, if not three, generations. G's therapist at Third Way Center was a very well brought-up young woman who felt that "dressing professionally" was important and set her apart from her clients. But this family thought of her as "stuck up" and felt it would be impossible for her to understand the pressures that poverty and illness had brought them. When she changed her appearance and could speak more like someone who also had come from a humble background—which she had—the family responded with openness.

b) Housing

Housing" has as much to do with the specific neighborhood and location as with the dwelling itself. A family and client who live in a gang-infested neighborhood will have vastly different concerns from a family living in an exclusive gated community. Thus, it's important for a therapist at Third Way Center to have a general acquaintance with the map of the state and the city that the client and the family are from. Small towns are not Denver, trailer parks are not small towns, and Five Points is not the lofts and high-rises of downtown. Where, exactly, all the family members live is sometimes difficult to determine, since many of our clients have families not only all over the state but in other states as well. And they tend to move often.

It is best, as soon as possible, to visit where the family lives. Third Way Center therapists have gone to visit families in nearly every state in the country, including Hawaii. Even before a visit can be arranged, the client can provide a description and, often, a drawing of the layout of the house. How many bedrooms? Where are they located? Where are the bathrooms? How does traffic flow within the house? This information is crucial, for example, where the client may have all the symptoms of sexual abuse, but no abuser or direct evidence of abuse can be found. It could turn out that abuse occurred because of the living space, where the client witnessed—visually or auditorily—sexual activity, at a very early age and against their will, as mentioned in the previous section.

> **Example:** When H came to Third Way Center, it turned out that her entire family—three adults and four children besides H, two of them adolescents—all lived in an apartment where they shared two bedrooms and one bathroom. Sleeping quarters were assigned rather haphazardly on a rotating basis. The mother had a number of boyfriends, who came and went without H's having

any control over the various relationships. There was nowhere for her or her siblings to go when arguments, sometimes of a violent nature, occurred or when sex happened. Safe boundaries were not a major consideration there. Passes for her to go home were delayed until this issue could be resolved, because exposure to explicit sexuality and violence since early childhood turned out to be the source of her PTSD.

A visit to the home can be telling in other ways, too.

Example: G came from a family of what appeared to be above-average means. The father was a full partner in a respected accounting firm; the mother was a stay-at-home mom with two children. Their son, G, was our client at Third Way Center. Besides some truancy and minor delinquent acts that had brought him to the attention of the authorities and landed him in the youth corrections system, it was difficult to determine what the problem within the family might be. In the family meetings, there was some mention of concerns over "environmental contaminants." These "contaminants" had caused the family to move very often and abruptly. When the therapist visited the home, she discovered that there was not a stick of furniture in the whole apartment. The family changed apartments, clothes, and cars every two to three months because of their certainty that, otherwise, they would be poisoned. In truth, G was trying to get help for his parents. It was the parents who were traumatized and delusional.

Visiting the home can reveal volumes, often more easily than asking questions. Thus, the therapist should not be afraid to ask permission, politely and kindly, to visit their home. One visit can save a lot of work! Again, it's important to gather all this information with an open, nonjudgmental mind, keeping in check all the prejudices one might have as a therapist about how families should live and keep their homes. The visit has to be conducted with great respect for the family and with much empathy for their particular socioeconomic circumstances. Bear in mind that it is the act of "doing"—going to the home and reaching out to family members—that enables the therapist to establish an alliance.

> **Example:** P was a Third Way Center client with severe symptoms of sexual abuse. His cousin, V, was also living at Third Way Center. The abusers were their biological fathers, brothers to each other. The paternal grandparents were very involved with both clients but denied that their sons had anything to do with the abuse. We visited the grandparents' home, a tiny bungalow in West Denver, which was absolutely crammed with pictures, statues, and artifacts of the Virgin Mary. Grandmother explained that it was the Virgin Mary who would protect her sons from sexual abuse by their biological father—abuse that had occurred in that very house. Thus, she fervently believed that they could not possibly have been abusers themselves. This visit opened a whole new avenue of discussion with the fathers and the grandmother about their sexual abuse. Both fathers had suffered, and the grandmother's feeling of total helplessness was clearly expressed in that house, where only her deep faith sustained her. She

had had nowhere else to turn with what she saw as inevitable. Our visiting her in her own setting, being understanding of that faith in her own sanctuary, enabled her to open up and made her an ally. With her help, both her sons could be approached and involved in the treatment process of the two boys.

Families are imperfect. The client's, the therapist's—*everyone's*—family is imperfect. As the therapist inquires and travels through every aspect of a family's life, it is helpful to remember this truth and keep it firmly in mind. It will make a nonjudgmental and cooperative approach possible and enable the therapist to elicit the help from the family that the client will need in order to heal and recover from trauma.

BIN 6.

Development History

WHETHER THE CLIENT has met all the developmental milestones (and to what extent) often provides a clue to when the trauma occurred. And it *always* determines what the client's sense of justice will be. In other words, justice, which restores the client's ability to grow, will always take place within the framework of the developmental stage in which the trauma occurred. It is the injured child within the adolescent who will need this particular and singular justice, which is specific to that child alone. Thus, the needed justice is not the same justice that the adolescent or the caretaking adult—or even the therapist—might deem appropriate. And it is most certainly not the justice system's idea of justice. Therefore, noting what milestones were missed will not only provide a clue to when the trauma occurred but will also make it easier to work with the client on what he or she sees as real justice for the trauma inflicted. Missing this crucial point is one of the major reasons why so many of our clients are not satisfied with the justice that has been meted out to the abuser, even if it is perfectly understandable and fair justice in the eyes of adults (including the therapist).

It is also necessary to determine the client's developmental progress in order to assess what role genetics or illness may also have played in missing milestones. It is genetics and illness that cause our clients to be so much more vulnerable to trauma in the first place. This determination begins with taking a careful prenatal history—a history of conception, pregnancy, delivery, and the first six to eight weeks after delivery. Alcohol, for example, has a great influence on the client's neurodevelopment. Illness in the mother influences development of the client. The birth process itself and a low Apgar score at birth would delay development and involve serious disruption of feeding and sleeping patterns. Another factor that can influence and sometimes delay developmental milestones is a bad overall mother-child fit.

For instance, a very passive mother would have difficulty bonding with a very active and demanding child.

> **Example:** When P came to Third Way Center, the therapist took a thorough family history. Doing the genogram, the therapist quickly discovered that this was a family consisting entirely of females—very kind and gentle females who all lived peacefully and happily together. Then, during a brief marriage, one of them gave birth to a son. Since boy children are typically not like girl children, the women all found P's exuberance—his need to explore, climb, and fight imaginary battles with stick swords—disconcerting and abnormal. They thought him unpleasantly aggressive. Although there was deep trauma in the form of sexual abuse in this child's life, the bad fit between mother and child made the process of trauma recovery most difficult and had to be addressed and resolved first. This seriously interfered with his attachment to the mother figures in his life, and their attachment to him, ultimately leading to serious acting out and

problems with self-esteem. This would have been the case even if there had been no other trauma in P's life.

Attachment or nonattachment, as well as insecure, inconsistent, or indiscriminate attachment, begins at this first stage and will determine the course and type of therapy. It is probably easiest to use Erikson's stages of development as a guide. These stages are described below.

Stage 1. Basic Trust versus Mistrust: Age 0 to 1

The caregiver does or does not meet the child's needs. The basic strength in this stage is hope. The child sits, crawls, vocalizes, and differentiates itself from mother or caregiver. The task to accomplish here is to learn that you can trust someone to come and help you if you are in need, but also that sometimes you need to wait. The child also needs to learn to *mistrust*. Some of Third Way Center's clients have had multiple caregivers during this stage of life after being taken from their mothers and placed in foster homes. They are distant or attach indiscriminately, and when trauma is added, they may become increasingly averse to close and trusting relationships. Or instead, they may become indiscriminately trusting. The trauma, when it occurs at this stage, is preverbal. Thus, it is not really amenable to this particular form of therapy (i.e., the six boxes of trauma resolution), since the process involves a lot of talking and some conceptualization. Also, what restorative justice might mean to a six-month-old child is mostly unfathomable. If, on the other hand, serious trauma occurred in a later developmental stage, then even though a disruption occurred in the development at this first stage, the boxes, by their very nature of being a schematic, are age appropriate to the stage when the trauma occurred. Therefore, trust is not an absolute necessity in completing the six boxes. The fact that this is a drawing and does not necessarily involve closeness to a therapist makes it very user friendly to many of Third Way Center's clients with serious attachment issues.

Stage 2. Autonomy versus Shame and Doubt: Age 1 to 3

Independence begins. The child can leave the caregiver for brief periods, learns to say no, and learns to walk and talk. If the child is thwarted, self-doubt begins, as does shame in dealing with others. The basic strength at this stage is will. The task to accomplish is to believe you can do things by and for yourself and get a little help. The child is learning to deal with doubt and to be ashamed when Mother disapproves. Trauma during this stage often leaves the child easily shamed, feeling that just about everything is their fault. Wanting independence but forever feeling disapproved of, they throw temper tantrums when thwarted. This sounds remarkably like adolescence, of course, and a great many clients at Third Way Center are stuck in this phase of development. As noted previously in this manual, a good example of this is the boy who believed that his mother's death was a suicide caused by his birth and his general "badness." He acted very much like a willful, shamed 3-year-old. His mother's suicide had indeed occurred when he was 3. He talked about and reacted to her death, even thirteen years later, as a 3-year-old would: everything was his fault, but because it was so overwhelming and unmanageable, he could respond only by huge temper outbursts whenever he was even slightly shamed or thwarted.

Stage 3. Initiative versus Guilt: Age 3 to 5

Self-directed activity begins. Parallel play shifts to cooperative play, and the child begins taking the initiative in seeking cooperative play. The child begins to pick out its own activities and pursues them. If the child is thwarted, self-directed activity will suffer through life. The basic strength here is purpose. The task to accomplish is learning to cooperate with others, being able to initiate play, and feeling guilty if hurting others. This is another stage during which many clients at Third Way Center suffered serious abuse. They feel deeply guilty about what they see as their "willing participation" in the abuse. Because they "enjoyed" either the sexual activity or the benefits their abuser provided for them, they are absolutely convinced that they were complicit and, hence, cannot "blame" the abuser or demand justice, no matter how sad and angry they get.

> **Example:** Y had always been quiet in his special-issues group, where sexual abuse was being discussed. When asked why, he said that if the group only knew "how bad" he really was, they would not want to speak to him. He was astonished when others in the group also admitted that they had, in fact, enjoyed the sex and yet still felt that what had been done to them was abusive. He had struggled in secret with his profound sense of guilt.

Stage 4. Industriousness versus Inferiority: Age 6 to 11

Task completion and exploratory play with other same-age children become the main focus. School and friends are of major importance. School becomes the center of activity. Parent(s) and teachers have to work together. The basic strength is competence. Tasks to accomplish are working at play, trying out roles, studying, having friends, testing out what it's like not to be the best at everything. This is where most of the clients at Third Way Center are really least competent. The abuse invariably has isolated them and restricted their range of activities and friends. Most of all, it robbed them of this stage of life. School is not the center of their activities; friends are elusive; secrets have taken center stage.

> **Example:** L put it best one day when asked in group why sexual abuse of children was not okay. He said, "Ever after that, I could only think of sex and I had no time to play." Thus, he never learned to practice growing up, either, and never met this stage's requirements in particular. He felt incompetent in social interactions with peers, was awkward in his attempts to engage peers in play, and spent a lot of time alone.

These four stages are the major developmental phases that the therapists at Third Way Center are interested in. These are the most vulnerable stages of development, and they are the ones whose outcomes are almost exclusively determined by others (parents, teachers, friends, neighbors). They are also the three major stages of development where the clients at Third Way Center are developmentally arrested and when their abuse occurred.

In the following eight stages, the individual has more control over the environment, and the individual is the one responsible for crisis resolution in each stage. Many of our clients have just barely—and only partially—arrived at this next stage, badly injured during previous stages and, hence, unable to complete the tasks of those earlier stages or the stages to come.

These first four stages also, of course, are the stages that our clients' parents and family members have (or should have) mastered. For family therapy and in evaluating family members for strengths that can be used in the client's behalf, carefully noting these stages can be tremendously helpful in determining the competence of the adults in the client's life and healing. Conversely, it is significant if the family members, too, have failed to master any of the first four stages of development, whether because of illness or because of their own trauma.

Stage 5. Identity versus Role Confusion: Age 12 to 18

Despite their being injured in previous developmental stages and not having successfully completed the tasks of those stages, most clients at Third Way Center, in one form or another, are very much in the midst of this stage, too. Unfortunately, physical adolescence, with all its attendant problems, sets in whether the client and the family are ready or not. Adolescence waits for no one! The major task in this stage is identity formation, which goes hand in hand with individuation and separation from parents. Forming a good self-image may be difficult when there is major trauma and humiliation that took place in much earlier stages. The difficulty of the task is compounded if the client has major disturbances in identity, and identity confusion, along with having to deal with childhood trauma. As a matter of fact, sexual abuse in earlier developmental stages makes identity issues even more difficult to resolve and can itself cause major identity confusion. If the abuser was of the same sex and much loved by the client, sexual identity confusion sometimes develops.

And, of course, the other major developmental task to be accomplished in this stage, namely separation, is made impossible by the ties that bind the victim to the abuser. This is the tie that, in the trauma work, must be broken or repaired so the client can move forward to the next stage in life.

The basic strength in this stage is fidelity, or genuineness. There is something very genuine about adolescents and their fiercely determined, biologically driven push toward health. It is the one stage in life that not only makes trauma resolution possible (because of the ego dissolution occurring) but also makes the formation of a new, healthier self *necessary*. If the therapist can tie into this drive toward growth, conflict resolution is possible and the process is much easier. Thus, having a client who is rebellious, loudly unhappy, complaining, and restless is actually an *advantage*. It is this very unhappiness that will make the client amenable to change. It is the defiant, restless adolescent, loudly proclaiming his or her profound rage and disappointment, who is looking for relief and resolution.

So . . . how to distinguish this from phases that nearly every teen grows through? It is the *frequency* and the *persistence* of this anger, to the point of self-harm, that make it significant and related to trauma rather than to mere "growing pains." At that point, not only the inner traumatized child is present, but so is the much more competent adolescent, who is demanding resolution and growth.

It is the compliant client, quietly self-destructive and stuck in early-childhood trauma exclusively, who is difficult to engage in the process of trauma resolution. These clients, with their internalized symptoms, are the most discouraged and need the most effort from the therapist to start therapy. In them, only the traumatized, hopeless child is present. A good example is the adolescent girl, mentioned earlier, who would behave well for months on end and then act out by self-harming, without any apparent precipitating event.

Stage 6. Intimacy versus Isolation: Age 18 to about 35

Rarely if ever have any Third Way Center clients even come close to this stage developmentally (despite having reached it chronologically). This stage requires the person to undertake productive work and establish intimate relationships with significant others. Otherwise, they will be isolated, which is so often the case in the clients we see at this age. Often, this has been severely impaired in the parents, also, thereby depriving the client of adequate role models. Often, because of trauma, the parents, too, have failed to find intimacy in their lives. Thus, they, too, are often lonely and disconnected. The basic strength in this stage is love.

Example: When D came to Third Way Center, she was 20. She had spent most of her adolescence in over fifteen placements and in hospitals for psychiatric and medical reasons. She had made over twenty suicide attempts by eating broken pieces of razor blades and jumping off high ledges. After trauma therapy using the process of the six boxes, she found herself, at 21, bewildered about peer relationships at college. She had missed her entire adolescence and was often tempted to go back to "being sick" rather than face the daunting task of catching up. Many questions of development still needed answers: "Who and what are friends?" "What is empathy?" "What do I want to be?" "What is dating all about? And how do you find a date?" "What do I do with all this free time if I can't spend it planning a suicide attempt?"

Stage 7. Generativity versus Stagnation: Age about 35 to 55
The task here is to guide and teach the next generation. Most of the client's caregivers have not been able to achieve this task, leaving the client with no one to bond to and learn from. This is also generally the age of the abuser when the trauma was inflicted. Since the basic strength of this stage is love, it makes sense why so many of our clients are so seriously deficient in love—and why the abusers so claim to love their victims. They have chosen a child to be intimate with, often have no job, and themselves are arrested at much earlier stages of development. Most parents of our clients are in this age group, and their children's trauma work very often stirs up unresolved trauma issues in them. At times, they themselves have asked to work the six boxes. Although the work isn't about *their* trauma, this should be offered to them because it will be easier for the adolescent client to do the work if the parent can,

too. Often, parents are angry and hostile to the process because they never achieved justice (or even thought it possible).

Stage 8. Ego Integrity versus Despair: Age about 55 and Up
People look back on their lives either with satisfaction or with despair, anger, and resentment. Most families we see have one generation after another looking back in helpless despair on their own failures and the failures of their offspring. Therefore, wisdom, the basic strength of that stage, is sorely missing. Even so, it is still a good point to bring in the grandparents. They themselves may not have achieved this stage (or maybe any other stage of adulthood), but they do have at least the wisdom of hindsight and may be able to help the family and the client right old wrongs. By helping the next generation free itself from the cycle of abuse and trauma, they themselves often feel a sense of justice.

The sixth through eighth stages apply to our evaluation of family members. The first five apply to the client and are particularly telling about where the developmental process became interrupted and at what developmental stage the client operates, especially under stress. Many parents of Third Way Center clients are also seriously arrested at earlier developmental stages since they, too, have often suffered the same abuse as the client. It is enormously helpful to the therapeutic process for them to know what those stages are.

> **Example:** In the process of trying to deal with T's destructive behavior, it became apparent that he and his mother seemed very symbiotic. They both seemed to be struggling with issues of shame and autonomy. Mother was easily shamed if even minor difficulties in her parenting style were brought up. She would become frantic, almost suicidal, when she had to look at any of her behavior as contributing to her son's difficulties.

She even enlisted other family members, who traveled great distances to defend her. She was extremely proud of being the breadwinner in their family, keeping her son and husband dependent just to prove how well she could manage. With much empathy from the therapeutic team, and great care never to shame her or challenge her autonomy, she finally did reveal disturbing imagery about her own abuse from about age 2 to at least 5.

The examples above should make clear how important it is, when doing family therapy, to recognize all the developmental tasks that each family member has either achieved or missed. In addition, we must consider accomplishment of the tasks of the first five developmental stages, which are the only stages applicable to our client. These two evaluations, taken together, will give the therapist all the necessary information that will allow therapist, client, family, and the entire treatment team to embark together on the trauma healing process. There will still be surprises and unexpected obstacles, but new information can be more easily assimilated once a framework is in place.

The above process of taking a thorough history can seem—and often really is—tedious. It would be so much more fun to jump right into therapy. After all, that's why most of us became therapists: for the treatment, the solving of people's problems. Most of us didn't go into this work to be meticulous, but we are indeed eager and willing to start the next section, which is all about the treatment process. Before we begin, though, a word of caution: there are no shortcuts.

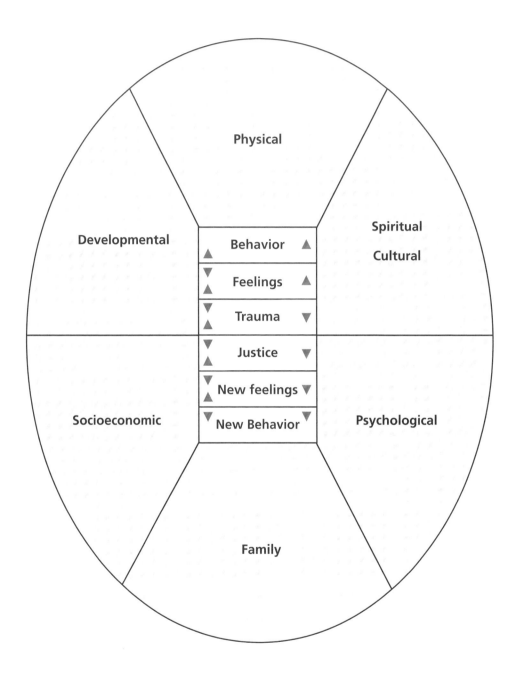

The Six Boxes

The Six Boxes: Six Steps to Trauma Recovery through Restorative Justice

Preparatory Work: Getting the Team Ready

Finally, it's time to begin the therapeutic process in earnest—or so it seems, at least. The therapist has collected the data and formed alliances. Though the therapist has made diagnoses and has a good idea which developmental stage the trauma occurred in, this doesn't mean that the process of collecting more and more data into the six bins should end—or, indeed, that it ever does. Most therapists would really rather just start at this point. But only now that all the pertinent information has been collected and the terrain ahead seems clear is it time to introduce the client, the family, and the entire treatment team to the six boxes and the process whereby trauma can be healed. A copy of the six boxes should be given out to all participants in the therapeutic process. (See Appendix 1.)

Chances are, this will meet with considerable resistance, largely because it often involves having to contact members of the family who may have lost custody to Social Services. Or there may be a restraining order against the perpetrator, or the family may be protecting the perpetrator. There is also the fear of entering unknown territory, of perhaps stirring up unpredictable behavior that could prolong the client's stay in the system or, worse, lead to dangerous acting out. The fear most often voiced is that the process of getting justice will provoke the client to act out violently. It is helpful to point out once again that (1) the particular act of justice that will restore the client's sense of fairness and freedom always takes place only in the context of the developmental stage when the injury occurred; and (2) the appropriate justice is an injured child's justice, not an adult's. The "getting even" is that of an injured child stuck in a particular developmental stage of childhood. Violent acts by adolescents are committed by the *rage* in the adolescents, after they are old enough to have formed the opinion that the world around them is an unjust and predatory environment, where there are only predators or prey. And they have always been the prey. The child within them has always been prey, but now it is the adolescent who is fighting back. That rage originated in untreated, unexamined abuse. And it is that rage—not the sad sorrow, shame, and resentment that children harbor at the time of their actual abuse—that leads to violence.

Why the Six Boxes
The six boxes aren't the only way that trauma can heal, but they are *a* way, one concrete way. It is the very concreteness of the boxes—the fact that teen clients can draw them, look at them, and write in the spaces— that gives them a feeling of hope that adults actually know a way, a process with a beginning, a middle, and, best of all, an end of therapy. Resolution is possible and even, perhaps, comprehensible. And because it is drawn in box form, even developmentally delayed clients can understand it. Also, at Third Way Center there are clients in various stages of this process, and they take hope from each other, for they can see the progress a peer has made. Clients are helpful with each other in making continuous adjustments and suggestions for how to improve

the process of the six boxes. Thus, the process is very fluid. There is much revisiting of all the steps. The boxes have perforated borders to help remind both the client and the therapist of this. They also have arrows that point in the direction the therapy should proceed, while allowing for regressions.

It is most helpful if the outside professionals, such as the case-worker, client manager, and guardian ad litem, are cooperative. Most of them, if they have not worked with us before, are skeptical of the concept of this kind of restorative justice "for" the clients, whom they see as needing only to *give,* rather than receive, restorative justice in their communities. But either way, restorative justice is about penance and redemption for harmful acts committed. Sometimes, the outside professionals see it as "coddling" or "giving excuses" for the client's bad behavior. People want to believe that "the past should stay in the past" and that "digging up old hurts" has no purpose, that thinking and talk-ing about the past only makes people feel worse. Sometimes, though, referring professionals are resistant simply because they had previous clients with us who, for whatever reasons, did not have the outcomes they hoped for, in the time frame they wanted—regardless of how far the clients came in the process of healing their trauma.

Indeed, if a strong, healthy individual incurs trauma—even early childhood trauma—biology and nurturance may have made it possible to simply wall off, put aside, forgive, or ignore that trauma. Such cop-ing may make some strong individuals tougher, stronger, and more resilient. But what if they can neither forget nor forgive? Many of our clients and families fall into this category. Moreover, they have innu-merable biological, genetic, social, and psychological deficits. Though these deficits most often are not of their own or others' intentional mak-ing, they nonetheless make the client terribly vulnerable to trauma. It is impossible for those clients to overcome their trauma on their own—often even with previous help by many well-meaning, caring professionals. Talking about the trauma has been tried many times, but they cannot forgive and forget. They are too wounded and too vulnerable. Or, as some research appears to have shown recently, they are biologically *unable* to forget anything that ever happened to them. At any rate, they have never, even in small ways, learned to get any kind of justice for themselves. What the strong have done for themselves since childhood—to speak up, get heard, get fairness, get a measure of justice, "get even"—the weak have never experienced. This is what we are here to teach them.

Preparing the Therapist

But before we can teach this to our clients, we have to be sure that we as therapists know the process intimately. When I first explained the six boxes and how they work to a friend of mine, he was suspicious and didn't buy my assertion that it worked for just about any problematic behavior. He challenged me, and I asked him to name a behavior that troubled him. He said he had been drinking way too much coffee, and this caused many arguments between him and his wife. I asked what he found so bothersome about that. After some thought, he said that it concerned being told what to do, which made him feel "childish" and made him feel that he had to be oppositional. I asked him who in his past had made him feel this way. He got angry, because he knew immediately (as I did, since I had known him a long time): he had a very bossy mother. It's interesting to note, though, that he then felt somehow that he had to "fix it." He had several long talks with his mother about this subject.

And it's no easier for the therapist to have to engage in this same process of admitting dysfunctional behavior when the therapist is the one acting out. It is important that the therapist, at one time or another, have to experience this realization personally. Anytime the therapist behaves problematically, the team should initiate this process. The most obvious occasion is when a countertransference is present. Clients' bad behaviors have a great way of stirring up the therapeutic personnel. The therapist's problematic behavior in response to the client deeply disrupts the therapeutic milieu and makes daily operations difficult—often impossible—and the therapist quickly becomes frustrated and upset. They want to make the problematic behavior disappear as soon as possible and, preferably, be the client's fault, just as the client wants it to be the therapist's fault. Fortunately, at Third Way Center, we operate on a team basis. It is the team's responsibility to point these issues out, discuss them honestly, and help the therapist who has acted out go through the six boxes to resolve the countertransference. It will teach the therapist the all-important point that to have empathy for the client, one must have empathy for oneself. It is also good to remember that blaming the client for the therapist's reaction and bad behavior has been tried on the client before, by previous treatment personnel, and—most often and most frustratingly—the client then has tried to blame the therapist. It didn't work then, either, and only resulted in an endless round of acting out and tit for tat with no solution.

Preparing the Client
The client will not entirely comprehend this process at first, so it has to be explained in simple, easily understandable terms. (See Appendix 3.)

1. The overall view starts with a general consensus that it has been impossible to go from bad behavior to any permanent good behavior. No matter how much the client was punished or went to jail, it has not happened. The behavior might have lessened in its severity, but its cost to the client, family, and society has still been great. And if the client is stressed, the behavior usually pops up again. A story of how animals are trained versus how humans learn is helpful here. We don't housebreak a dog by asking him how he feels! He gets trained by punishment and reward. Human beings, however, require much

more than punishment or even reward. As a matter of fact, overwhelming research shows that punishment does not extinguish bad behavior successfully or permanently. Humans are sentient beings. They feel deeply and are often ruled by what they feel, making it impossible to alter their behavior even with the best intentions. Most adolescents love this concept and understand it only too well.

2. It is not always clear to the client that they feel anything at all at the time they get into trouble. They sometimes don't even believe that their behavior gets them into trouble in the first place. But a discussion of how feelings drive behavior might help set the stage, allowing a conversation about how this might be true for the therapist as well as the client. And this can open the door to a conversation about how something unresolved drives those feelings—something bad that may have happened a long time ago. That *something* is the trauma. Maybe, it is even many "somethings" that have to be sorted out. Someone once said that therapy was like wandering into an aspen grove: we see many trees, yet they all have the same root system. Similarly, we have many symptoms but only one root system. But unlike an aspen grove, the injury just sits there and festers and wants to be acknowledged. And not just acknowledged—it wants *justice*. It wants the person who caused it to do something about it, thus restoring a sense of fairness. All our clients know only too well that they have had to pay and are still paying for their own bad behavior. Why should it not be just as true for the people who have injured them? Only when that question is answered and dealt with can new feelings emerge. And those new feelings are never as nice as might be expected. It is important to warn the client, the family, and the team that the treatment is not yet over or resolved. That is because doing something about the trauma is not a simple thing. Initially, there is elation and a new self-confidence, a lightening of the client's burden. But then, doing something about the trauma also brings with it much sadness over the losses: loss of childhood and loss of trust, sometimes accompanied by guilt. Only when those feelings are resolved is it then possible for new, more productive behavior to emerge. But basically, it is Third Way Center's contention that without restorative justice for and by the client, health and chances for a productive life are unlikely.

3. The therapist will not make the client revisit the trauma in excruciating detail or suffer without help and support. After all, the client has already relived their trauma in their own mind, alone and for years. Many a therapist has retraumatized them. It is realistic, however, to know that at times, restorative justice may cause pain to family members and, often, to the perpetrator.

4. The process is fluid. The boxes do not have solid lines or barriers. It's okay—probably even necessary—to go back and forth between the boxes. The client cannot just put information, memories, and practices into each box and be finished. Each action that is problematic is an opportunity to rework the steps again, box by box. The crucial stage is box 4.

5. Give the client, the family, and everyone on the client's team a copy of the drawing of the six boxes. (See Appendix 3.) The client should always keep a copy and should be asked to fill it out at different stages of the therapy. The more they can familiarize themselves with it, the more they practice. The fact that teens are used to filling out forms and doing homework makes this easy for them. It fits into developmentally appropriate tasks, and they are amazingly willing to use this very visual material in the therapeutic process. It feels as if it isn't really "therapy," which they are resistant to anyway on principle—and not only because of previous disappointing experiences. The same is true for families. To them, too, it feels more of a learning experience and something very tangible.

6. Most adolescents value independence, and since adolescent development pushes them toward attaining freedom, it is typically easy for the adolescent client to accept that this process might help them accomplish this. At least, it gives the client hope of avoiding further punishment and severe inconvenience—by working through the process of the six boxes. Basically, selling the idea of restorative justice is not difficult, although selling it as being *for* the client takes a bit of faith by the client and the entire treatment team. Sometimes, the adults in the client's life don't believe that the client deserves justice after having offended so much. Sometimes—often, actually—the clients themselves firmly believe that they do not deserve to get restorative justice. It is helpful to explain that developmentally, it is impossible for a child to have empathy for others, to give justice to others, without having received it first for oneself. In simpler terms, we have to have our own wound kissed before we can kiss another's wound. When a child is very young and gets hurt, the primary caretaker soothes, comforts, and shows the child warmth and empathy. In time, the child imitates the caretaker and begins to show the same behavior toward others, if only to please the primary caretaker. In time, however, and with reinforcement and reward, the child grows up to internalize this behavior and learns to be an empathic and caring adult who responds to the distress of others. This is so very basic that even a young child can understand it, agree to it, and see how empathy is learned. And yet, hardly a client at Third Way Center has experienced this!

Adjunct Therapies

This is a process that will also draw on other therapeutic techniques. At times, everything from cognitive behavioral therapy to insight-oriented therapy will have to be employed. Chances are that in boxes 2 and 4, very strong and difficult feelings will emerge. It will be helpful then to start the client in a dialectical behavioral therapy (DBT) group to help manage these feelings. Small-group therapy, which generally works well for adolescents, is also especially helpful in this process. That's because it is useful for various members of the group to be in different stages of obtaining and resolving their justice, thereby giving the ones just starting out hope and examples of how to accomplish this.

Psychotropic medication not only often relieves the structural issues that make trauma resolution impossible, but also may help the client deal with the onslaught of overwhelming anxiety that the process often causes. Psychotropic medication may have to reach therapeutic levels before the six-boxes process can begin.

> **Example:** When C was placed at Third Way Center, he was overtly psychotic. He demonstrated all the symptoms to make a diagnosis of schizophrenia necessary. Also, he had been abandoned by his biological mother and had been severely beaten by her until she lost custody of him. Anytime trauma issues came up, he would run away and would be found with homeless people living under the bridges of Cherry Creek. First, we had to take care of his psychosis and find the right medications. He stabilized very well on Haldol, and as he did, he stopped running and was ready to find his mother. And find her he did, but unfortunately, she was dying from chronic kidney disease. Even so, he got to spend quite a bit of time with her, discussing the past, asking about her care of him, getting her to cry and apologize. She introduced him to other family members and gave him back a sense of belonging. That was her gift to him, and that was his Box 4—his restorative justice. When she died, he mourned her appropriately and deeply without decompensating. He then moved, slowly and with new family support, into a new life centered in who and what he was to become.

It is important for the therapist at Third Way Center—and the whole treatment team, for that matter—to know that the entire process of completing the six boxes may not always be possible during the often all-too-brief stay at Third Way Center. When completion is not possible, it is then more important to understand the process, work out what might be a reasonable restorative justice, and determine how it might change the life of the client if it could be accomplished. A significant number of clients in our system either could not or didn't want to complete the boxes. But after they left Third Way Center, they continued to consider what they had learned. And they were able, either by themselves or with the help of other therapists, to complete the boxes. It is also possible to get clients to practice the six boxes for minor bad behaviors that even the client finds troublesome. Such behavior may be as insignificant as chewing gum too much, for example. Success with these "practice runs" is helpful in giving the client courage to tackle the work on more devastating traumas.

> **Example:** Third Way Center received a letter recently from a client who had been a resident over ten years ago. No one even remembered when she had been here. She merely wanted us to know that while she was a resident, she had learned the six boxes but had not wanted to practice or apply them to herself. But as she got older, she realized that her behavior was indeed determined by what had happened to her. So she wanted us to know that she had found herself a therapist, taught her the six boxes, and gotten well. As unusual as that is, she actually thanked us. She never mentioned what her therapist thought of being "taught"!

Acting Out and Justice

This brings us to one more principle to talk about when starting the six boxes. It is a way of getting justice restored without having to act out impulsively, thoughtlessly, or harmfully—or, indeed, even wanting to act out. It teaches becoming aware of what hurts us, and allows the practice of thinking and discussing what can or should be done about it. It teaches us to name the trauma and the wishes. It teaches us to examine all the secrets out in the open. I often help the client and the involved team see that trauma is like Freddy Kruger in the movie *Nightmare on Elm Street*. The more you run from "Freddie" (the trauma), the more it pursues you. Only by our turning toward it, facing it, naming it, does the nightmare become manageable.

Healing trauma is no different from what happens with ordinary injuries in ordinary families. Ordinary parents teach their children early and often how to discuss the injuries they receive from the world around them, how to sort out what is worth standing up for and what is not. And, more importantly, they teach their children how to get justice, first from siblings and parents, then from playmates, then from school, then from authority. They teach normal successes and failures in that endeavor. Also, the more a child gets to practice this skill, the better the child will become at the process and the better the child's self-esteem will be. No victims ever had confidence—in themselves or others.

> **Example:** Having been a grandparent for a number of years now, I have been able to see this process right up close. I have three grandchildren, ages 8, 6, and 4. And as with siblings everywhere, there is an ongoing succession of injustices inflicted by one upon another. The offended party will invariably approach Mother and complain of the grievous wrong they have just suffered.

Their mother, my daughter-in-law, whose training is in the financial field, not in psychotherapy, will turn to the child and ask quite seriously, "Well, what do you want to do about this?" A conversation will then ensue about what is fair or unfair and what can or cannot be done about the situation. Since I have no influence over this, it has been fascinating to see the resolution of these conflicts, and how simple the solutions are!

This method works for big as well as little traumas, just as in the normal developmental process. In some ways, it is the difference between giving a hungry person a fish to eat and teaching him to fish. This is often hard to remember when there are serious time constraints on how long we have a client in residence, and tremendous pressure from the outside team just to get the client a job and get them "settled" rather than resolving anything. It takes great courage in both the client and the therapist to teach this process when it should have been taught a long time ago. And, of course, there is nothing in the process of being caught up in the social welfare system that would heal the wrongs done to the client and the family. Rather, the emphasis is on the wrong done *by* the client and the family. The six boxes will, with a bit of luck, reverse this process.

Developmentally, the exercise of boxes 1 and 2 in particular causes the client's prefrontal cortex to develop. It introduces the issue of self-awareness, mindfulness, and, in some ways, DBT's idea of radical acceptance. The boxes make the client look into the mind, and this helps develop empathy—at least, empathy for oneself. Adolescents like the fact that naming the behavior, writing it into box 1, makes it theirs. To name it is, in some form, a way to *tame* it. Trauma derailed normal behavioral and emotional growth. And trauma can also be named and tamed and dealt with—by settling the issue of justice.

BOX 1.

Behavior

HERE, finally, begins the real work of therapy. These are the phases that got us here:

- collecting the necessary data
- taking care of the underlying structural psychologi cal deficits that might make the process impossible
- explaining the process, not only to the client but also to the family and—very importantly—to the entire team involved with the client: as social services, youth corrections, legal representatives, mentors, and anyone else involved
- alliance building

During those important phases, the process itself should have built an alliance between client and therapist, and that therapeutic alliance will be the basis of this, the first step of therapy. Clients and families can hear difficult, troubling observations only from a therapist they trust and do not feel judged by. One way for a therapist to achieve this trust is to remember that absolutely no one in the whole wide world screws up their life on purpose. All actions, at the time we engage in them, are perceived as relieving tension and "fixing" whatever is wrong. This may not encompass the entire truth, but it is certainly a good working premise, especially with adolescents. Observable bad behavior is a tremendously valuable diagnostic tool because a client will tend to engage in *the same* bad behavior each time. When clients regress under stress, the behavior they go to is repeated over and over with every regression. That behavior is also always a developmental regression. Thus, when acting out, the client will behave like a much younger child. And the age they regress to is the age at which the developmental arrest occurred following the most serious trauma inflicted on the client. This, together with the data provided in the history, is one of the most important clues to what the trauma (the injury) was and when in the client's life it occurred.

There but for the Grace of God Go I

Not that people in general, or therapists in particular, are all that different. Nearly all people, under some particular stress at one time or another, have behaved badly. Maybe the occasion was a stressful holiday, a party with too much going on, an argument that went out of control. And the funny thing is that on each of those occasions, the bad behavior was much the same. Indeed, a friend or significant other—spouses are especially good at this—might observe that the one behaving badly was "acting like a 5-year-old"(!). Or it could be that the actions were those of a 3-year-old. It doesn't matter; the point is, it was a regression to an earlier developmental stage, and it was always a regression to the *same* earlier developmental stage. If the team can help the therapist see what might have taken place during that particular stage in his or her life, and the therapist is open and willing, they, too, may experience the joy and pain of healing an old wound. Whenever the issue comes up in my seminars, the response on the part of the therapists is a universal recognition of this—and, often, an eagerness to get going on this process right then and there.

Observing Behavior

It may seem obvious to every adult on the team that the client's behavior has brought nothing but punishment, pain, and trouble. But it certainly is not obvious to most of the clients who are placed at Third Way Center. In all the time the facility has been operating, no client I know of has ever come into this placement saying that their own behavior was what got them into trouble and got them placed here against their real wishes. Most clients would rather talk and argue endlessly about how their behavior, though deemed inappropriate by the world, was the only real choice of action they had at the time, given all the circumstances, if only the thick-witted therapist could understand all the circumstances. Moreover, the clients often argue that they have been provoked into this sort of behavior by the annoying actions of others. And in some ways, in light of their trauma, that is perfectly true! (Only not so true in the simple way they see it.)

It is only through the alliance that the therapist has developed with the client during the foregoing process, and through the persistent empathic agreement that no one is here to argue about the client's guilt or innocence, that getting through this phase is even possible. It is the process of making a truthful observation, in a nonjudgmental way and within the therapeutic alliance, about their behavior and its effects that allows the client to hear that observation. And only then can the client recognize that a behavior was unsuccessful, resulting in punishment and all manner of trouble for everyone concerned. The goal is for the client simply to be able to accept that whatever the reason may be, the behavior brings with it a boatload of trouble. Seems simple enough, right? But given the oppositional nature of both adolescents and adolescent therapists, it's difficult to accomplish without getting lost in an argument. The theme to stress persistently is that this is not about guilt or innocence. It isn't even about "taking responsibility for your actions," which is most certainly something the client has heard. This is actually what they have heard most of their lives within the system, at home, in school, and everywhere else. Indeed, they've heard it so much, they are fairly well convinced that the therapist just wants them to admit their "guilt."

Cost-Benefit Ratio

But the therapist must firmly and empathically stress that the *only* interest the therapist has in the bad behavior concerns the sheer *unprofitability* of that behavior. The cost-benefit ratio is simply not good. In this, there should be no blaming and no moralizing, either spoken or implied—not even so much as a raised eyebrow. There should be only sad caring, sighing, shaking of heads, to make the client understand how sad, not angry, everyone is that it's not going well. The milieu therapy done by Third Way Center staff lends itself really well to this approach. In the milieu, innumerable opportunities arise for the therapist to observe variations of the same behavior that got the client into trouble and into placement in the first place.

It is exactly at this point that the genuine, nonjudgmental empathy of the therapist becomes the conduit, the way, to the client's acceptance that there are painful, often barely perceived feelings that underlie and drive the behavior. So it is the *affect* of the therapist that allows the client to get into box 2: the feeling driving the behavior. This is the second phase of the healing process.

Rather than show exasperation—or, failing that, perhaps *in addition* to showing exasperation and anger—the therapist would do best to show the client empathy and even some sorrow. Empathy because it is this kind of acting out that gets the client into trouble; begets punishment, further abandonment, and dislike; and only adds fuel to the anger within the client. Clients will say that acting out this way does make them feel better because they at least took action when they hurt someone else by disobeying the rules. The client took action, and that seems to be empowering and rewarding—for the moment, anyway. But, of course, the wrong person got punished for that action, and that punished person (i.e., the therapist) will punish back. Was it worth it? Either at that moment or a bit later, this is the crucial question to ask. Was it worth it, and did the relief last? Was the result not, in some way, only that they managed to revictimize themselves? The temporary relief never lasts and never will. At the very least, the question will rankle and stay in the client's mind, and lots of arguments will ensue. And this introduces the all-important question of cost-benefit ratio. There are costs, and it is those costs that eventually bring the behavior into the context of the entire treatment process.

The Trouble with Empathy

It may be particularly difficult to show empathy for the trouble that teens get into for their behavior when that behavior is directed toward the therapist. Adolescents have a way of being uncannily correct in the unpleasant observations they make about their therapists, their parents, and other caregivers. It's even harder when the Third Way Center therapist is working hard in the milieu, trying to keep it organized— get a meal on the table, say—and has to deal with a client who has just decided to take an illegal smoke break because his father, yet again, didn't show up for the family meeting, bringing back all the feelings of previous abandonments. And that adolescent has decided, in the midst of this generalized chaos, to tell the therapist in no uncertain terms what is wrong and "peculiar" with the therapist, how he or she just the other day also broke promises and is a "liar." And the several other clients on hand agree loudly. It is very hard to be empathic in such moments. It's hard even to remember what the instigating client was hurt by and what precipitated the outburst.

This process of maintaining empathy is equally difficult in family therapy. Again, though it may be blatantly obvious to the therapist that the family, the foster family, or even the caseworker or client manager is engaging in dysfunctional behavior affecting the client, it is never so obvious to the involved parties. Accomplishing this awareness is no easy task, especially not with people outside the agency. Again, we hope that the process of getting necessary, infinitely detailed histories from them has forged a bond, an alliance, that makes it possible to bring up the subject of bad behavior being unprofitable. It's important to leave aside all judgments of whether the family's dysfunctional behavior is morally, ethically, or legally unacceptable. The only thing that matters is that it brings the family much unhappiness and causes a great deal of trouble.

> **Example:** Client K had been working hard on her trauma with her team and all the professionals involved. Then she developed serious diabetes, which required a great many doctor and clinic visits because of her many symptoms and the difficulty of regulating her blood sugar. This greatly exacerbated her serious anxiety disorder. Staff responded appropriately both to her medical condition, with prompt attention, and to her anxiety over her physical condition, with empathy and methods to decrease her anxiety. But the lawyer involved in her case became terribly anxious over the illness and shared this with her client, whose anxiety then skyrocketed. The heightened anxiety resulted in more unnecessary trips to the emergency room, not only frustrating the staff but also taking precious time away from the client to work on her fears of dying from the illness. It certainly was a lousy cost-benefit ratio, but difficult to address with the lawyer, who had a very difficult time looking at her own behavior.

Looking for Help

Once again, nobody screws up their life on purpose—not even an adolescent, even though it often seems that way. No amount of punishment can have greater force than the feelings that push the behavior. No one makes a shambles of their life and brings the wrath of others down on them intentionally. Everyone is only looking to feel better. This is a universal truth, and remembering it makes it easier to stay away from judgmental statements.

It is also obvious (though often forgotten) that human beings, particularly adolescents, are notoriously difficult to train. Unlike with dogs, horses, monkeys, and elephants, no matter how much humans are rewarded or punished, if there is internal unrelenting psychological pressure, they will have to act it out. This is especially true of adolescent humans. It often helps our clients when the therapists can talk about that and explain how so many people before have tried simply to push the client from box 1 to box 6, with little lasting success. So, if that can't be done despite everyone's fervent wishes and hopes, and if we accept that nobody screws up their life on purpose, then there must be *something* that keeps success from happening.

From this understanding, it follows that feelings push behavior. Most adolescents end up acknowledging this, even though having to admit it makes them mad. Then they generally act out. And then, finally, they can talk about that issue. Then they can acknowledge that *strong* feelings push *strong* behavior.

Punishment

None of this, of course, removes the need to impose consequences for the client's bad behavior. Throughout this entire discussion, every therapist reading it has been anxiously waiting for this section, asking nervously whether bad behavior should therefore be tolerated. It should not, of course, but consequences can and should be quickly and efficiently handed out and should fit the crime. And preferably, the therapist should take the opportunity to point out once again how self-harming that behavior is and how loath the therapist was to impose the consequences. It is best for the therapist to complain bitterly that so much valuable time now has to be spent on thinking of and then enforcing consequences. Consequences are much easier to accept *after* this discussion than before.

Note that at this point, the client is not even being asked what the feelings might be that demand and always result in this or that particular unprofitable behavior. But as soon as both therapist and client agree that it is sad and unprofitable to engage in bad behavior, it is time to ask what the client feels before, during, and after engaging in this behavior.

For example, illegal drug use is often the most obvious "bad" behavior, and every therapist knows that it is a form of self-medication. But self-medication for what? Answer: always for a bad feeling. This is a great opportunity to move into box 2 with the client. After the empathy and expression of sorrow over how unhelpful it was to get caught and punished once again for using drugs, the opportunity arises to ask about what the client may have been feeling to be pushed into illegal drug use. One thing is certain: the client always knows that doing drugs made things feel better. So—after the consequences—off into box 2 we go.

BOX 2.

Feelings

Feelings Drive Behavior

Where there is strong behavior there are strong feelings. Before box
1 is even finished, the therapist now should have an agreement with
the client that there are, in fact, feelings that are troubling. As for what
those feelings might be, adolescents in general don't give very useful
answers to that question at first. Most often, they tend to feel that the
therapist and other treatment personnel have been simply too annoying and that if they had not been so terribly annoying, the bad behavior
would not have occurred in the first place. And most often, they have a
point: adults *are* annoying. They make too many demands and ask too
many stupid questions—or so it seems to the client. Not being overly
defensive about this point helps smooth the way for an actually useful
discussion around feelings.

Despite the client's vociferous complaints, it's important to stick
with the question about what feelings accompany the bad behavior.
Nothing is lost by acknowledging that the therapist is annoying. It is
still possible to maintain the position that strong behaviors have underlying strong feelings. It might also be pointed out that the behavior
was there *before* the meeting with this particular annoying therapist. So

what are those feelings? Start with the feelings at the time of the bad behavior. Though it needs to become the persistent question, how and when to ask it, and how to get the client or the family to stay with it, becomes the therapeutic skill.

Often, the feeling is painfully obvious to the therapist but confusing and obscure to the teenage client. It is important not to name the feeling but to wait for the client to be ready to name it. Waiting for them to blurt it out may take patience. It also takes persistence and even the willingness to be a bit annoying. When they are angry or upset, they most likely will find it easier to blurt out painful, often very *old* hurtful feelings. It's difficult for them to lie when they are angry. In the welter of sometimes abusive enraged yelling, themes of old injuries are there to be heard if the therapist can listen empathically at the time.

For example, the question of what feelings are present might elicit this answer: "You made me mad. I feel really mad. I am really mad. *Therapist:* "What else?" *Client:* "Frustrated with your stupid questions. You are stupid, a f****** a******!" *Therapist:* "Frustrated like often and with lots of people? Besides me, who?" Invariably, there is a long list of people who made the client mad. Included in that list, of course, are more and more people with a close and intimate connection to the client. The more the client yells, the closer they will come to the people they are really angry with.

> **Example:** A had just had a great disappointment when his father did not show up for the scheduled family meeting. It was dinnertime at Third Way Center, and instead of helping get a meal on the table, A decided to take an illegal smoke break, and another resident went out with him. Therapist B was infuriated, harassed, and divided about who needed her attention the most. She opened the back door and started demanding, in an

angry, frustrated tone, that the two come back into the house instantly and take up their chores. An argument ensued. Of course, B realized that the situation might become explosive, so she stopped and quietly asked the client who had accompanied A to go back inside, told the mental health worker to look after the others, and stepped out to join A. She told him she was sorry his father didn't come. He cursed at her and yelled at her. He was very much in touch with his anger. He was mad at her and, of course, at his father. She said that if it truly helped to be mad at her, he would already feel better, and how sad it was to incur further consequences. Was it worth the cigarette? Did it make him feel better? His father still wasn't here. How often had that happened before? He started telling her. She said she would spend time with him after dinner to discuss this further and in detail. He came in and ate his dinner. It was very important to him that she later honor her promise to talk with him about how it felt when his father continually abandoned him. Together, they had entered box 2.

Managing Feelings

The next step is to help the client tolerate these strong feelings without acting them out. It may be helpful for the client to join a dialectical behavioral therapy group to learn to tolerate and separate strong feelings. At any rate, it is always helpful at this stage to use DBT principles, in a short or long version, as an adjunct therapeutic model. DBT not only helps one tolerate strong feelings but also allows the client to recognize a greater *variety* of feelings. The teens we see tend to have a very restricted range of feelings they are consciously aware of, and are often stuck at just one predominant, preferred, and all-too-familiar feeling. And mostly, that feeling is one of overwhelming anger to mask sadness. Particularly male clients at Third Way Center seem to have boiled all their feelings down into one: rage. Anger became for them the only safe feeling they could ever express. But that anger stands in for a lot of more complicated feelings, which can be told only to a trusted staff member. Or it may be permissible to express other feelings in small-group therapy, where another client has advanced to being able to exhibit more nuanced feelings and is showing the way.

The issue of self-soothing also comes up. Few traumatized people we see can do this without engaging in further bad behavior (mostly illegal drug use). DBT is very helpful in that it teaches a number of useful ways to calm oneself. It provides exercises in how to do this. Even if a client is unable or unwilling to be in DBT group, the therapist can teach and use DBT principles in their simplest form with the client. The therapist can certainly acquaint the client with a wider range of feelings and some simple self-soothing techniques as outlined in DBT. This is important because the next two steps will likely stir up even more strong feelings. Once again, it is important to explain to the client, the family, and the treatment team that this is likely to be a difficult time for the client.

There is usually a maze of feelings, leading to a plethora of traumas. The client will try to deal with those traumas that are easiest to tolerate and have the least meaning. And our clients have such a wide variety of traumas, it's difficult to know which of the feelings to pursue. From the history, it should be clear which is the earliest developmental stage in which the client is stuck. But then we must also figure out at which developmental stage the client is *most* impaired. This should have become apparent through observing the behavior the client exhibits when regressing under stress. We explored this under box 1. This will lead us to determine during which developmental stage significant trauma was inflicted on the client. These three pieces of data may not always match. It may be that illness has caused delays at an early stage, whereas trauma has caused much more severe delays at later stages. A carefully taken history should have elicited data on both illness and trauma, and careful observation of the client under stress should have given clues about the stage of development to which the client regresses. Also, throughout the client's history, there is much evidence, and the records are full of observations about the client's feelings and behavior. The therapist can state that previous observations noted this or that troublesome feeling. Often, the client tried to confide about those feelings to a trusted staff member, but it was never resolved. Might that feeling still be there?

Empathy for Self

At this point, the client typically can tolerate the therapist's asking where these feelings might have originated. Sometimes, unfortunately, the persistent answer is that the therapist is the one at fault, and the source of the strong feelings. Then it may be useful to ask who the therapist reminds the client of. Or sometimes, it can be helpful to show how the therapist is annoying only by inches, whereas the client is reacting by yards and yards. Both humor and sarcasm are helpful and, for adolescents, seem to soften the impact that raw emotions have on them. And feelings have to be softened and soothed for adolescents since their normal lack of ego controls makes them feel much more intensely and powerfully.

The most important point in doing box 2 is that this allows for the introduction of a most important idea: that the client must have empathy for her- or himself. The empathy that the therapist shows for the unrelenting difficult feelings that push the client makes it easier for the client to have self-empathy. Once again, it is helpful to remember the fundamental fact that if one cannot have empathy for oneself, one cannot have empathy for others. We have to learn to be sorry for ourselves before we can be sorry for others. Very often, our clients tell harrowing stories of having been explicitly forbidden to show any sorrow for themselves. This is the fundamental sticking point for many of our clients, who ask plaintively why they should show empathy for their victims when nobody showed empathy for them. They leave out that they need and yet never had empathy for themselves. None of our clients have had good or even adequate early experiences with this. When severe trauma was inflicted on them, there was no one to feel or express empathy, no one to express sorrow. In fact, most of the time, no one even *believed* the client. Instead, when the victim started to victimize others, the system was quick to demand that the adolescent show empathy for the victim—a task that has proved all but impossible to enforce. Contrary to all belief, within the juvenile justice system, genuine empathy cannot be demanded.

Consequently, the next questions will come up: how often, and then how long, has the client felt this way? Time spent on this subject makes it a bit easier to ease into the next question, the crucial one that invariably has to follow: where did these feelings start? Often, the struggle of recognizing that feelings are not generated out of thin air makes the client connect the feelings to previous situations, leading inexorably to the original trauma.

This is not a stage or a box that adolescents stay in for very long. The intensity of feelings is too strong, and the need to find a solution too demanding. In some ways, this makes the move to box 3 easier. Or sometimes, the move back to box 1 becomes irresistible to the client, and client and therapist have to start all over again. The arrows in the boxes go both ways. Acting out in response to feelings just seems so much easier and feels so much more familiar. But once the journey through boxes 1 and 2 has been written down, this becomes a visual aid to staying with it—a visual aid both for therapist and client.

Example: Q was a very compliant young woman at the most restrictive of all Third Way Center's facilities. She had been in a great many treatment centers, always for sudden severe acting-out episodes: escapes with sexual promiscuity and drug use, noncompliance with probation, followed by months-long periods of tranquil and pleasant acquiescence. At the Lowry center, where a lot of acting out went on around her, she was unusually compliant. So her discharge planning began, and all her therapists and her client manager declared her ready to go to a much less restrictive setting, where she would have her very own apartment. Everyone, including Q, seemed pleased. Then she ran away. Once again she exposed herself to danger. This time, when she was caught and returned to Lowry, her therapist pursued the behavior by asking persistently for the feelings that were present when she acted out. What she revealed shocked everyone. She began to talk about her sexual abuse. There was indeed a reason why she had behaved so badly, why she felt so sad about herself at times. She began to talk about things that triggered her overwhelming feelings of rage and unhappiness, which she felt could be handled only by the excitement and danger of being on the run. She had not only named her feelings and connected them to her behavior but had actually seen that there was indeed a cause for why that happened. Was it perhaps reasonable to examine, name, and tame that trauma? She thought it might be worth a try.

The move from box 1 to box 2 is made possible by the empathy and respect the client learns to show for her own feelings. Encouraged by

the therapist's empathy, the client finds acceptance of complicated feelings possible. It even becomes possible to wonder, know, and connect
those feelings with events in the past. The agreement reached then is
that feelings do indeed originate in things from the past, particularly
from unresolved issues, called traumas. It follows that those traumas
have to be investigated. What seems so obvious to a therapist, namely
that trauma wounds the victim to the point of causing mental illness,
is by no means obvious to the client.

> **Example:** M came to Third Way Center insisting that
> he was "crazy" and must be "schizophrenic." He was
> obsessed with this and with a lot of other odd thoughts.
> He had been tried on several antipsychotics and even
> on OCD medications, without the slightest improve-
> ment. His persistent complaints and obsession with
> the idea that he was schizophrenic made it nearly
> impossible to take a history from him. It took weeks to
> get to the six bins, when that should have happened
> within the first two weeks. What did finally emerge,
> however, was a history of serious physical abuse by his
> stepfather. This stepfather was still in the picture, and
> M's entire treatment team had planned and pushed for
> him to return home. But he was terrified to go home
> and felt so trapped that he convinced himself he was
> "crazy." One day, purely by accident, a client who had
> been at Third Way Center but now was in college and
> doing well came in to say hello, and he asked about this
> client. She told him that she had survived her trauma
> through getting justice. It wasn't this statement that
> astonished him and changed his life; it was her say-
> ing that her trauma had made her "crazy." He strug-

gled with this discovery, turning it over and over in his mind, till he thought that perhaps he, too, had trauma that had made him "crazy." He then began to tell his therapist how terrified he was of returning home, and began at least thinking about doing his own justice work. It had taken him months before he could go to his box 3.

BOX 3.

Trauma

A Word about "Trauma"

We use the word "trauma" liberally throughout this manual, and it is the surest term for therapists to convey to each other what they are dealing with, what they are trying to figure out and heal. But it is a word that should never, *ever* be used with the client and the family. It is a "therapist word." It is an off-putting word to clients—a word that they often don't understand and that conjures up images of physical injury. It is a word that, when used, will most certainly put distance and fear between the therapist and the client. It is a word that neither the client nor the family will take to. Unlike "justice," which is near and dear to their hearts, "trauma" is a frightening word. Every therapist has to figure out what words to substitute. Using such words as "bad things that happened," "secrets that went on," or even "injury" is much more helpful. Some useful substitutes for "trauma" are "upheaval," "distress," "stress," "strain," "pain," "anguish," "suffering," "upset," "agony," "misery," "sorrow," "grief," "heartache," "heartbreak," "torture," "ordeal," "trial," "tribulation," "trouble," "worry," "anxiety," "nightmare," and "hell." These are the words that should be showing up in Box 3, and these are the words the therapist should use with the client and the family.

Types of Trauma

Throughout this manual, we are talking mainly about five types of trauma occurring in childhood:

- sexual abuse of a child, whether by seduction or by force, by a person in a position of trust
- physical abuse of a child by a person in a position of trust
- emotional abuse of a child by a person in a position of trust
- neglect or abandonment of a child by a person in a position of trust
- existential trauma, such as severe chronic illness or disability, of a child

A combination of these traumas may be present, but there is always one, from one of these five categories, that damaged the child most deeply and at a specific developmental stage. It is the developmental arrest at that stage, and the return to that developmental stage during periods of stress, that allow the therapist to sort out which trauma is the significant stumbling block to further development.

Knowing and Facing What Happened

Most clients at Third Way Center have had innumerable placements, where they have had to recount their traumas innumerable times, with no changes and really no one knowing what to do about them, until they grew discouraged and angry. By the time they come to Third Way Center, they are no longer interested in retelling their story one more useless time. Thus, we really have two kinds of clients: those who have never told anyone what drives their acting out, and those who have told it way too often. Either way, the resistance to therapy is powerful and the fear of being retraumatized is intense. That fear should be equally intense in the therapist. The intent must be never to hurt the client or the family again, never to be idly curious about details of the trauma, but always to be respectful and patient with how much the client and the family are willing to reveal and how much they can tolerate. For the process of healing, not every detail of the trauma has to be relived, recounted, resuffered.

But deep in the brain's limbic region is where our memories reside. On the left are explicit, factual memories, and on the right is where we store autobiographical memories. This is well described in a recent book, *Brainstorm,* by Daniel J. Siegel. It is this autobiographical memory that causes the affective distress seen in box 2, triggered sometimes by even minor environmental annoyances. Helping the client face more of the factual memories, providing more factual evidence of the trauma, may help the client grasp more clearly why the things that have happened have caused so much trouble. It may help to integrate the two memories, which normally happens in the hippocampal region of the brain.

Getting the client's voluntary cooperation for this process, and their explicit permission to get more factual data, will be wonderfully helpful in getting them to agree to work through the entire process of the six boxes. To then introduce this data when the client or the family is ready becomes the *art* of therapy—the knowing when the time is right and the empathic support is there. Great care must be taken not to overstimulate or overwhelm a client with the emotional turmoil this joining of factual and autobiographical data can cause. Great support and adjunctive therapies have to be available at all times. This supportive system must be in place and planned for when taking the history.

> **Example:** An example of what *not* to do is the case of
> S, a young man who had a lot of vague autobiographi-

cal memories of his mother being sexually inappropriate with him when he was 4, and of being removed from her care at that point. No other evidence could be found, and eventually he stabilized a bit and was to be moved to a foster home. Two days before the move, his treatment team received the verbatim transcript of his mother's admission to the police of what she had done to the client. Because his therapist felt he had no time to work with S around this, he simply gave S the transcript. Reading it flooded the client with all the fears and darkness he had buried in his unconscious. He became overtly psychotic and required intensive therapy and medication.

Connecting Trauma to Boxes 1 and 2

What is significant in all this is that the clients of neither group, by the time they arrive at Third Way Center, have any clue what trauma has to do with painful feelings or with unprofitable, troublesome behavior. Most of our clients are sure they would not act out or be irritated if the outside world would just leave them alone. The second group, the ones who never told anyone about their trauma, are often the most quickly amenable to the questions: "What in the past has made you feel just like that? What does it remind you of?" It is consistently amazing that after an outburst of bad behavior with a storm of feelings, there is an opportunity to explore this next step. It inevitably leads to the trauma that has most affected the client—the one injury, among all the injustices done to them, that bothers them the most. And, of course, all trauma needs naming.

Rarely if ever is the trauma a single event in a Third Way Center client's life. It is usually multiple injuries of the same kind, inflicted over time. Thus, the client feels a tremendous sense of hopelessness about having to look at the profound injustices that were inflicted. The clients often shout, yell, and complain bitterly of once again having to acknowledge the depth of the injury, guilt, and shame. It is best not to overly retraumatize the set of clients who have told their traumas so often. There is little to be gained from having them recount to the therapist in any great detail the injury done. The only thing that matters really is that the client see how the past determined their present and future behavior via the feelings that keep coming to the surface over and over again. And, most importantly, the therapist must be reasonably certain that the trauma occurred. That is, the symptoms the client has must correspond to the trauma the client says has been inflicted, and the behavioral regression and affect must fit that event. The symptoms should have been clearly elucidated in the process of taking the history.

For example, girls who have been sexually abused in childhood have markedly low self-esteem, often are promiscuous, and lie constantly about even minor things. They often act and look very sexualized in almost all their relationships. Boys who have been sexually abused tend to be extremely combative, sexualized (especially when angry), and ready to fight at the drop of a hat. It is interesting that during the two times in history when sexual abuse of young boys particularly was socially and culturally acceptable—classical Greece and Renaissance Italy—both those epochs were marked by endless violent physical feuds, secret violent betrayals, and ambush murders among males.

Obstacles

One area in this box will need some extra work done. Many clients feel that because they seemed to have submitted to the sex and enjoyed it (or enjoyed the benefits they gained from the abuser), they are therefore just as guilty as the abuser. It is common for children to believe that if they did not put up a fight or suffer utter revulsion, they must be "bad" and guilty and, therefore, cannot blame the abuser or have any empathy for themselves as the victim. When this is the case, a compassionate and caring discussion around the power differential that existed between the abuser and the victim is important and has to happen. It is also helpful to point out that everyone likes being given presents and that really, unless it was rape, everyone—even a child—likes sex. Much to the client's surprise, everyone likes sex: young people, old people, short ones, tall ones, fat ones, skinny ones. It has nothing to do with culpability. Special-issues groups with other victims who felt this way and who overcame this obstacle are most helpful in taking away much of the shame and the feeling that it must have been the child's fault. This belief is often fueled by the abuser, who convinces the child of their irresistible attractiveness and their specialness.

Another set of clients also exhibit all the symptoms of post-traumatic stress disorder, but they insist that there was no trauma. Some clients have engaged in "bad behavior" only periodically, done their time in various juvenile detention centers, and come to us truly believing that the bad behavior was random. They have learned their lesson and need only learn "independence skills" and get a job. Unless the client is discharged within a very short time, invariably they begin to act out again. When they do, it's time to point out to them that nobody screws up their life on purpose and nobody acts out without a very compelling reason—it simply is too expensive, too unprofitable. Sometimes, it is much harder to convince the entire support team and the family of this than to convince the client, and this may indeed be the most frustrating and time-consuming part of the entire treatment process. Sometimes, this is so difficult that eventually, the therapist—especially if young and inexperienced—will give up. They end up convincing themselves that maybe, just this one time in all history, bad behavior really did mean only bad behavior, without reason or purpose beyond the client's simply having been "bad" or made "bad choices."

Example: O was placed at Third Way Center with the plan that he was to learn independent-living skills quickly because of his long stay in detention. He was to get a job, emancipate, and leave. He had been a model detainee who had "learned his lesson." He got a job quickly, did his chores, and followed the rules—at least for a while. Then there were conflicts with peers he lived with, with staff around taking too much time off and around conflicts at work, and he got back to illicit drug use to ease the discomfort. He went back to detention. During the postmortem on the case, it became obvious that he had given many hints about his psychological distress and was anxious a lot, especially around sexually abused youngsters among his peers. Nobody wanted to ask, and so nobody asked.

When the therapist consistently and empathically pursues whatever might underlie the feelings that push the behavior, the client begins to look at the past that they have been trying so hard to avoid. The usual lame excuse is that they "can't remember." But this means only that they think it is *not worth* remembering, because even if they do remember, nothing can be done anyway. *It happened a long time ago; there's no use in confronting the pain all over again; nobody would believe it anyway (since nobody believed it then); it will only upset everyone because they don't want the people they love to get into trouble; the family has forbidden all talk about "it"; it's my fault anyway; it wasn't that big a deal; it wasn't really "abuse," because nobody forced me into it; the abuser really cared specially about me; I was a bad kid who deserved whatever was meted out.* And on goes the endless stream of reasons why the abuse cannot or should not have had anything to do with the intense outburst of feelings that resulted in the bad behavior that got the client into trouble. Once again, the fact that they are behaving badly and that their behavior is stuck at a particular developmental stage is helpful to the therapist in asking about what might have happened around that age. The process of taking a thorough history once again comes into play, along with a close observation of what developmental age the client exhibits most when anxious and in trouble.

Consent to Treatment

It's important to let the client sort out which, of the reasons they give for having kept their secrets, is the most dominant, and how it came to supersede the need to talk about the trauma. Then comes the therapist's empathic statement that if it had indeed been possible to suppress the trauma, there would be no acting out. Then the client has to weigh whether it is worth continuing to suffer and suppress, acting out the rage and sadness, rather than undergoing the suffering involved in dealing with the trauma. Ultimately, it is the client's decision—an important fact to remember. It might be helpful to remind the client of the entire process of the six boxes and that nothing in box 4 will be done or said until the client and the therapist agree on it. They will not even be required to entertain the ideas in box 4 unless they want to. It is interesting, however, how many clients, once this "trauma-informed" process is discussed, will immediately go to talking about what could possibly happen if they do talk about their trauma. As much as they fear the next step, they sense the need for it.

The therapist has to accept that even if the client does not decide at this particular time to go beyond box 3—or even really to *enter* box 3—it is acceptable because they have been practicing with small traumas to get to boxes 4 through 6 and will be free to do so with their major trauma when they are ready. They need to know that they are safe to talk about their fears and suspicions. Their memories unfold slowly, bit by bit, not because they "could not remember" but because of their fears.

Help

Another point to remember is that in the history-taking process, the question of who can help the process was asked and answered. At this juncture, it is vitally important to involve those people. The cost-benefit ratio of facing the trauma versus continuing to act out is best discussed with them. Actually, this person often is a parent who also was abused, and once they realize that they will not necessarily be asked to undergo this process themselves, many see it as at least an opportunity to set the next generation free. When the entire family is afraid, that issue must be taken care of first, since it's a rare client indeed who can start (let alone finish) this process against the wishes of the entire family, no matter how close the alliance between client and therapist. The risk of a breach with the family is too great. Blood is still thicker than water, and the wise therapist never forgets this.

> **Example:** when I was in private practice, I saw a boy, age 13, who had been through a number of therapies for his aggressive and uncooperative behavior. He even had "rebirthing therapy," which was all the rage then. When I looked at the videotapes of the rebirthing sessions, I noticed that whenever he was asked the "reason" for his bad behavior, he would say he didn't know, and stare intently at his mother. She would smile. After I gained the mother's trust, she tearfully began to talk about the beatings she had given the boy whenever she was even slightly frustrated, thereby teaching him the violence he exhibited. Then and only then could the boy talk about it.

Multiple Traumas

Making an alliance with the family makes it easier to answer a question that often comes up: Which of the multiple traumas the client has suffered should the therapist start with? Ultimately, it is the client who determines this. It is the trauma that pushes the out-of-control feelings that, in turn, push the dysfunctional behavior. It is therefore also the affect—the feelings—that often gives veracity, truthfulness, accuracy, to which trauma is in box 3. The affect has to match what the client is recounting. If the affect doesn't match, further work is pointless until this is resolved. Just because a therapist *thinks* something is traumatic does not make it so. Of course, many times the clients have recounted their "trauma" so often, they seem desensitized to it. But if they continue to act out, *something* else is still driving them. Their symptoms and their developmental arrest have to match the trauma and the diagnosis arrived at in the history-taking process. It's important, then, to look further as soon as the client and the family can tolerate this and give permission.

> **Example:** W showed all the symptoms of PTSD when she was admitted to Third Way Center. She startled at the slightest noise, slept poorly, and had horrific nightmares. She also acted out all the time, sexualized all her relationships, and lied often, even about the most trivial issues. She repeatedly almost got expelled for having relationships with various boys in her house. When we pursued what affect might underlie her troublesome behavior, she was able to talk about feeling small and insignificant and good only at sex. With further exploration, she began to talk about how her grandfather had started sexually abusing her at around age 6 or 7. She recounted many details. The problem

was that nothing of what she said carried any significant affect. She merely recounted it as if she were talking about the weather. The history she portrayed did
not match the affect of the behavior she exhibited. And
in fact, when stressed by her peers in the milieu, she
threw temper tantrums like a 3-year-old. Luckily, her
therapist was very disturbed about this and simply kept
talking about the discordant affect. After much testing
and much denial, affect returned, with tears and then
the ability to talk about the events of previous abuse.
She became like a frightened 3-year-old again, and her
affect matched that stage. Even before the age of 5, her
biological father had abused her. The grandfather's
abuse had merely followed.

Thus, as in the above case, the developmental arrest of the client
helps determine which of the traumas is the one that disabled the client. Once again, this point cannot be stressed enough: finding the
most troublesome, most disabling trauma involves the gathered history, clinical observations, and matching, appropriate affect pointing to
what developmental age the client appears to be arrested in.

The *kind* of trauma the client has suffered matters greatly to the client and the therapist. What we seek isn't "trauma" generically; it is child
specific. Certainly, the behavioral fallout is often similar in children with
similar traumas. All adolescent acting out may look the same to adults.
But the pain, or perception of the injury inflicted, varies widely and is
completely child specific. Sexual abuse, for example, might manifest in
a client's grossly oversexualized behavior or language, especially when
angry. But lots of adolescents seem oversexed! Much of the real effect
of any abuse seems to be played out because of what the *child* perceived
to be the unbearable part of the abuse—which is not always obvious

to the therapist. That is, was it the lying, the betrayal, the pain, the hunger, or something else that caused the deepest injury, which will require justice, will need "fixing"? The seeming injury inflicted by any given abuse never seems to be what the adult therapist looking at it retrospectively would expect. This is another reason why recounting the details of the injury may not be as necessary as listening empathically and reflectively to the pain within the injured child. A good example of this is the young boy who was chained as a toddler and forced to eat out of a dog bowl. It was the *hunger* he felt that caused the greatest trauma.

Multiple Traumas: Repetition Compulsion and Transference Resistance

Most clients with unresolved childhood trauma tend to get retraumatized repeatedly ever after. It is easy to mistake these later traumatic incidents for the original trauma in box 3. But they are not the original trauma. They occur because traumatized children are easier to revictimize, or else they are repetitive efforts by the now more grown-up client to resolve traumatic issues from childhood. This latter reason is often difficult to sort out because it is an attempt by the victim to recreate the original trauma with someone new—typically a caregiver. This then becomes a typical transference situation. When the transference becomes the only thing the victim is interested in—that is, when all the people chosen by the victim are made to play the part of the abuser—the transference becomes a transference resistance.

> **Example:** When M, age 17, was referred from Wyoming to Third Way Center, he had already been in six foster homes and had been up for adoption at least once. Each time, he would enter the foster family with enthusiasm and great expectations. But then his old troublesome behavior would emerge. He would run away, use illegal

drugs, become disobedient and break the rules of the home, and eventually become verbally abusive when even slightly annoyed. This angry, hostile, challenging behavior was directed mostly toward his foster mothers. It is noteworthy that he had a long history of neglect and abandonment by his biological family. Between the ages of 2 and 5, he was repeatedly transferred from relative to relative. Traveling unwillingly from home to home, M was essentially unwanted and an extra burden wherever he went. When he finally entered the foster care system, he was quite sure that people would once again reject him and find him "too much to handle." So he quickly set about making sure he really was a burden. He did it both to test his new family and also to make sure that the inevitable came to pass. In his most recent foster home, the foster mother had indeed become verbally abusive toward him. After all his testing and taunting, she ended up thoroughly hating him, and she let him know it. When he came to TWC, it was easy to empathize with him over this, especially since he could be very charming and sweet. He then insisted that his "trauma" in box 3 was this last bad relationship with another disappointing foster mother. And for his box 4, he wanted to "get even" with this foster mother.

It is noteworthy that during M's stay at TWC, he was extraordinarily unempathic toward other victims of child abuse living with him on the unit. He and some of the staff had a hard time seeing that box 4 is not as much about revenge as about *justice*. He did not want to see how unjust and unfair it was both to him and to the foster mother that he had precipitated—even necessitated—the harsh treatment he was expecting. Moreover, he thought that his endless bad behavior should therefore be forgiven and forgotten. But all that bad behavior still required just atonement—as the Department of Youth Corrections confirmed. He still must take responsibility for that behavior. His repetitive bad behavior will, at the same time, require him to have empathy for himself as well as for the people that behavior was directed at. Neither they nor this most recent foster mother, who also felt terrible about her own bad behavior, were the original problem that M was struggling with. No amount of rage directed at random people will ever resolve the original trauma. His original trauma and, therefore, his original anger must be directed toward the first people who abandoned him and found him a burden and a trial at an age when it was clearly their responsibility to care for him, not his to care for them.

Since most of our clients are about to enter adulthood, it is important that they learn one of the sad but important bits of wisdom that adulthood brings: that it isn't hard to make the people around us angry at our behavior. This is especially true if they care or want to care about us. And it is then easy to blame them for their response to our provocation. This leaves us with *two* problems: the original irritation that caused the provocation, and the new problem of having to make up to the person we let our irritation out on. When this is observable (as in M's case), it may be a good point in the therapeutic process to introduce this concept. At the same time, M must go back and deal with when this process of feeling helpless and enraged started, and determine for himself whether the original abandonment by his family could be the original trauma.

The Therapist's Trauma

This brings up a crucial question: Is a therapist who cannot listen to his or her own inner child capable of doing this work? Certainly, a therapist who has no self-empathy finds this stage most uncomfortable and is tempted to try to prevent painful affect from welling up within the client or within the therapist. Most commonly, serious countertransference issues emerge. Therefore, it is most important that therapists themselves have had to show that empathy toward their own injuries and have gone through their own process of healing.

> **Example:** When client Q started dealing openly with her sexual abuse, the family members were often high on drugs during the meetings. Q's therapist became judgmental and angry with the parents for being "unresponsive" to Q's pain, just as the therapist's own father had been to the therapist's pain. And from that point on, the therapist refused to have further meetings and demanded that Q, too, cut herself off from her family "once and for all" until they "shaped up." This was against Q's wishes. This therapist had let her own inability to be empathic toward herself—her inability to solve her own trauma issues—get in the way of helping her client heal. This presents an excellent example of what countertransference can do to derail the process of healing.

Finding the Perpetrator

Somewhere in these three phases, it should have become apparent who the primary offender or perpetrator is. Then it sometimes becomes important to track that person down, check out their present status, and, if at all possible, begin a dialogue with the perpetrator. Of course, this is much easier said than done, because the entire team will be afraid and very much against it. Nowhere in the therapist's training has there been a course on how to do this or even encourage this course of action. It is less difficult, though, if the perpetrator is known to everyone and has already suffered legal consequences for the abusive behavior. (This is actually more often than not the case with Third Way Center clients.)

At the very least, the most significant people in the client's life will have to know early on what is being discussed and pursued. This invariably frightens the child, and issues of trust, both in the therapist and in the family, have to be addressed. The client will have to be supported, and this puts the therapeutic bond to the test. It is hard work, requiring great finesse and courage from the therapist. It also may require great persistence and great gentleness. It will seriously test the therapist's ability to be empathic.

As with the client's dysfunctional behavior, it is just as important to remember that the therapist's job is not to judge and that most likely, the perpetrator, too, has been abused. Perpetrators do not ruin their lives on purpose, either. Third Way Center's therapists are always astonished at how often the perpetrator, once no longer judged, is willing to participate in the process at least to some small degree. The family, too, when not judged but instead empathized with around how hard it is to handle suspicion and family cohesiveness, is often willing to discuss these issues, however painful. Families may do this more or less graciously or gratefully, but the message here is more important than the vehicle. Therapists should learn from the example above and try not to complain about this. Being able to think about possible resolution and maybe penance and justice is often relieving to families, too.

At times, the therapist, with permission from the client, will have to start allying with the family and start the dialogue with the family concerning the abuse. It is the therapist, not the client, who must do this, because if the client could have dealt with it alone, they would not need the therapist and would have been able to resolve it with their family by themselves. It is not reasonable, therefore, to expect the client to be of much help in this stage. The client is entirely too conflicted and can only give permission for this to take place (by allowing the therapist to speak to the family, allowing the therapist to track down the perpetrator). And the client can rightly blame the therapist if anyone gets angry or upset in this process. Then the therapist will have to resolve the ensuing conflict. But then again, the therapist certainly should be better prepared and have more skill than the client in family conflict resolution. It should be easier for the therapist than for the client to handle the family's anger and take responsibility for bringing up painful issues. That's where the whole purpose of having made an alliance with the family becomes crucial.

> **Example:** X has been discussed in this manual as having had to get permission from her mother to testify at her father's trial for sexual abuse of a minor (X herself). He was found not guilty despite his daughter's compelling testimony. The judge nevertheless lectured and severely reprimanded him and jailed him for being an illegal alien. X's therapist went to see the father in jail and began a dialogue with him about restoring some justice to X now that the threat of incarceration no longer hovered over him. During that meeting and in following meetings with both parents after his release, a long process of admissions to guilt and discussions around justice ensued. X said, "When I thought about confronting my dad, I never imagined it would take all this long work." Very succinctly put. She at least understood at that moment how difficult it is to get through box 3.

This is in contrast to healthier families, who may also face abuse of one of their members.

Example: An 11-year-old boy I knew announced at the dinner table, quite out of the blue, that he no longer ate hot dogs. When the family expressed surprise and asked why he had decided this, he said ever since his 18-year-old cousin had lived with them the year before. When asked what the cousin had to do with hot dogs, he explained that it reminded him too much of the cousin making him perform oral sex on him. The family responded with great astonishment, and everyone in the family came to therapy to see what could and should be done. This family reacted and faced box 3 instantly and as an entire family unit.

Again, it is most important to note the developmental phase in which the client shows deficits and in which the trauma took place, because it is within that context that the client will address box 4. It is the recognition and acknowledgment that it was a child, not an adolescent or adult, who was abused, and thus, it is that child who needs to determine what justice will restore life and future development! This bears repeating endlessly.

Reporting the Abuse
As in X's case, most Third Way Center clients have, in previous placement, reported their abuse, and the abuse was or was not founded. Third Way Center therapists need to check this out in great detail to know what has or has not been done. If the abuse has not been reported, then this needs to be done and will greatly influence the speed with which the client and therapist can handle box 3. The reporting process itself is often terribly traumatic for the client. On the other hand, both the client and the therapist may mistake mere reporting of the abuse for the restorative justice itself. It never is. It is merely a legal require-

ment. Reporting the abuse involves shaming the child, who was, after all, attached to the abuser. And it is not in any way related to the child's need to find retribution for the betrayal of that relationship. Reporting the abuse is satisfying only to the adult and, at best, (ever so briefly) sometimes to the adolescent.

BOX 4.

Restorative Justice

AL-ANON TELLS US, "Let go, let God." So does AA. And this advice seems to work for millions. But to make the benefits really stick takes continuous, unrelenting support. Whatever trauma is buried in that right limbic system gets triggered by stress, and if the person suffers from any psychobiological deficit, keeping that trauma under control, keeping it under wraps, is next to impossible. So the first step in box 3 is moving the trauma into the *factual, knowable* part of memory. And then there is still the need for conscious acceptance of that trauma, on the one hand, or for restorative justice, on the other. Most of the work of conscious acceptance should have occurred in Box 3.

Making Amends

But even under the AA tenets, the alcoholic must make restitution to whomever he or she has wronged. It's interesting, though, that this restitution is determined by the alcoholic perpetrator. At no time does it require input from the victims, or any thought to what their idea of restorative justice might be.

This, the victim's determination of what constitutes appropriate restorative justice, is the crux of this entire new process. This is the definitive "new idea" that Oliver Wendell Holmes speaks of in the open-ing epigraph of this book. This is the new concept for the clients. And it differs from their previous experience of slogging endlessly through boxes 1, 2, and 3, aimlessly recounting to therapist after therapist the sordid, painful, unbearable details of their trauma—trauma that has truly ruined their lives and that they haven't been able to do a thing about. Meanwhile, compounding the injustice, they have had to pay, with way too many placements and incarcerations, for the trauma they inflicted on others. And our clients are very aware of this. They have received lots of suggestions on how to deal with this. Most of these suggestions have to do with taking control, not letting the trauma ruin their lives, gaining control over the pain by using various techniques including DBT, self-soothing, cognitive behavioral psychotherapy, motivational interviewing, rapid eye movement therapy, any and all "trauma-informed or -determined psychotherapy, and so on. Well, the clients *would have* taken control if they could. They have tried and been encouraged to try, often by caring, loving people who thought their love for the sufferer would somehow be enough.

Recently, a series of prime-time television ads from the ASPCA has shown the plight of abused dogs. These TV spots have been heart wrenching and have caused many a heated discussion about how the abusers might be made to pay for hurting innocent animals. There are no TV spots for abused children. But it's interesting how similar the suggestions for helping the abused animals are to people's sug-gestions for abused children. Basically, the thought is, find them lov-ing homes and they will blossom and be cured. Those of us who have taken in abused dogs know that it isn't quite so simple and that suc-cessful reintegration into a family requires a bit of training from ani-mal experts. That's because not even dogs forget.

Our clients have had years and years to think of what they would like to do to their abusers—thoughts that are complicated by their conflicted relationships, with both the abuser and their own families. And no matter what punishment the system or the family may or may not have inflicted on the abuser, it was not the client's decision. As a matter of fact, the client was not even consulted, because the assumption is that the adult world knows what the proper punishment is for any given transgression. This might also be a problem for therapists, who feel that *their* idea of what should or should not happen to the perpetrator is the true restorative justice for their client. If the client's conception of restorative justice is not carefully monitored and kept acutely in the therapist's conscious mind, the client can't be open and honest about what justice they would like to see. The adolescent may then be too ashamed to tell the therapist that the "justice" the adult world has exacted is irrelevant to the child victim, is not age appropriate, and is downright unsatisfactory. In my experience, the therapist must have a close alliance with the adolescent client before the client is willing to talk about the *real* justice they want.

> **Example:** F was doing quite well at Third Way Center. Staff had found his father, who, after inflicting much violence, had abandoned the family and left it destitute when F was 7. The family disintegrated, and F's life became a series of placements and rejections. I had been following his case quite closely and watched him as he started to communicate with his father and told him about his life. Fortunately, the father, too, had grown up, and he responded with sorrow and apologies. F told me he had found his "voice" and that it had made him content. I asked him, "But what does the seven-year-old in you want?" A big grin came over his face, and without a second thought, he said, "I want him to play catch with me, and I want him to bring the ball like

he promised." Why had he never told his father? With a shrug and an embarrassed grin, he said, "Nobody asked me. And anyway, it was silly." Silly? Maybe, but that was what he wanted, and it was quite doable. He had judged his justice to be "silly" and "undoable," and it was actually very difficult to get him to ask for this particular justice from his father. It was the therapist who had to bring it up to the father and explore it first.

Obstacles to the New Idea of Restorative Justice

Most adolescents are quite judgmental and unempathic with the child victim within them. They would very much prefer that the child be quiet and disappear. They have little empathy for themselves and are used to being told that the child's complaining and importuning is just self-pity. Though that can be true, more often we see judgment on the part of the adolescents, who feel that it was their own fault, that they willingly participated in the sexual abuse or deserved the physical abuse. This is the secret they hang on to—the secret that often keeps them from being empathic. Lack of empathy leads to silence and secrets and the attitude that their fantasies about what they want to do to their abusers are childlike and "stupid" or "silly." Thus, lack of empathy keeps them from telling. Sometimes, it's easier not to ask about the victimized child within. But after the trauma injury is clear to the therapist and the client, asking what the client would like to do about it "in their deepest, most secret heart" is often the least painful way to elicit an answer.

Not that therapists can't be just as judgmental and impatient as their clients. If that question is asked too early without a thorough therapeutic alliance, it becomes unanswerable by the client, because the adolescent simply will not permit the therapist to get in touch with the injured child. Vulnerability is not an attribute that adolescents value much, to say the least. Thus, for example, when I put that same question to another client, whom I barely knew, I got a vague, evasive answer filled with a lot of "I don't know's." The next step would have been very tempting, experienced therapist that I was. I would have wanted to suggest to the client what the justice piece might be, and applied the "standard" practices that therapists generally have learned to think might help the client. One of the most common examples of these standard methods is to have the client write a letter to the abuser. Most often, that letter is not to be sent. Instead, it is burned or sent up with a balloon, in a gesture of renouncing the abuse. Though all commendable efforts, these are justice gestures invented by adults and superimposed on the client's child within, and make only the adult feel better. It's best to resist the temptation to offer solutions, especially in cases such as this, when the client really doesn't have an alliance with the therapist and hasn't even agreed yet on what the trauma may have been.

This is the second new idea and is even more important than the first (the idea of justice for the victim). This is justice determined by the victim—the punishment the victim wants to exact. The restorative justice that she or he needs always takes place within the context of the developmental stage during which the trauma occurred. This means essentially that a part of the client's development was arrested at the time the injury or abuse occurred, and that the justice the client wishes for must be appropriate to that age. It means that a 5-year-old's idea of what is "fair" or just is very different from the justice that a 3-year-old might want. Each developmental phase expresses its idea of "getting even" differently.

> **Example:** When H was admitted to Third Way Center, he arrived shackled hand and foot, with a guard on either side. He had had huge temper outbursts at the youth correctional facility: screaming, cursing, and

kicking things and people whenever he was thwarted or made to wait. When I saw him, I had already read his extensive chart and knew that his father had sexually abused him for a long time around age 4 to 5. The father had been convicted of sexual offenses, had gone to prison, and died there. When I asked H what was the matter with him, he cursed me roundly and told me exactly how stupid I was. I agreed and then told him I was puzzled because it seemed to me he had gotten justice with his father's conviction. So once again he told me how profoundly ignorant I was, because it was not *his* doing that got his father convicted. When I asked what he wanted, he told me he wanted to "piss" on his father's grave but that he had been told it was against the law and he would be locked up for it. I realized that the way 4- or 5-year-old boys express their disdain and assert themselves is often by literally "pissing" on people. We helped him with his wish. He did "piss" on his father's grave and talked to the grave, and this freed him and let him start to grow. His tantrums ceased when he moved into box 4. He clearly demonstrated that (a) he had arrested a good deal of his development at the age of 4 or 5, (b) the justice he needed was within that narrow developmental window, and (c) the justice needed had nothing to do with the justice that the adult world had chosen to mete out to his father. It is a lesson not to be forgotten.

It is terribly difficult for the adult therapist to actually see what a child's justice would look like. This often seems quite unfathomable to adults. And then there are the complications of what the client's relationship to the family was like during that particular developmental phase. This is important because the younger the client's age and the closer the relationship with the abuser, the greater the betrayal and the greater the effect of the trauma—but also, the greater the conflict between loving and hating the abuser. And once again, the therapist must not become judgmental. Words such as "abuse" and "abuser" must be avoided like the plague. It's best to stick to words that merely reflect the relationship the child had to that person. Heed the example of client F, whose father had been both cruel and loving. F never forgot, either, and most of all, he wanted proof that the loving father was back.

Almost all our clients both love and hate their abuser, although "hate" is perhaps too strong a word to use here. That is, unless the abuse was hurtful and violent, and even then children are attached to—or at least dependent on—the supposedly caretaking adult. And, of course, many abusers assure the child that whatever is being done is done in the name of love and that the child is "special" and has a "special" (i.e., secret) relationship with the adult. Alternatively, the abuser is much loved by someone such as the mother in the family and, thus, inviolate. So this part of the process is fraught with both great love and great sadness and anger. The therapist must be able to tolerate this ambivalence because only by accepting it and working through this will the client tell the therapist what the hurt child within has been ruminating on for years. After all, unfortunately, the hurt child is not the only one present. There is also an adolescent, with all of an adolescent's obstinacy and willfulness and need to be independent and invulnerable. It is this adolescent who often is most derisive and judgmental of the child who suffered the injustice, and who makes it hard for that child to speak.

Helpful Rules

Therefore, the initial outpouring of fantasies in answer to the question—*the* central question of this stage: "What do you want to do about it?"—

might be a mixture of childlike and adolescent musings. At that stage, it is important for the therapist to remember and, perhaps, to gently remind the client and the entire treatment team that restorative justice has four rules.

Restorative justice cannot be . . .

- illegal,
- amoral,
- unethical,
- or unhealthy.

For the most part, these rules are self-evident. Some of the wished-for justice that the victim wants to mete out may sound at times like all of these. It's the therapist's job to help the client sort this out.

> **Example:** When asked the question "What do you want to do about it?" S said with great glee that he wanted to find his father and ring the front doorbell. And when the father came to the door, he would pick him up and beat the tar out of him until he cried for mercy. Mind you, this was a very small, slightly built youth who loved Superman. With a bit of gentle help, he could see that although he loved the idea, it was probably not possible. And even if it were possible, what would happen to him then? If he could not be Superman, what would he want to be? What he settled on was that his therapist should confront Father and that his therapist's words would beat Father! Then Father would admit to S that he had done wrong. This example shows that although the justice is the child's, also present in therapy is an adolescent, albeit a badly injured one.

For over twenty years, I've listened to the answers to that central question, "What do you want to do about it?" That question has elicited a variety of astonishing answers that were far from breaking any of the four rules. And this is because it was a *child* who was abused, not an adult or even an adolescent. Often, even when remotely violent thoughts are involved, they are of a cartoonlike quality, and the adolescent client quickly recognizes that. And it is truly amazing how clear-cut and clearly thought out the client's ideas are about what penance by the offending adult would make the client feel better. After all, they have had quite a few years to work this out. It's just that nobody ever asked them.

> **Example:** When S was a child, his father had chained him like a dog and fed him almost exclusively out of a dog bowl. The father had been jailed. Third Way Center's staff shuddered at the humiliation the child had suffered. When S reached box 4, he announced that he wanted to see his father. His father had just been paroled, and there was much concern over S's safety. To his therapist's amazement, he did not want to confront the father, nor did he even want him to apologize. What he wanted was for his father to supply him with a sandwich that would last all day and that he could share with all the teens in his program. What he had felt at the time of the abuse was unrelieved hunger. His therapist went to see the father, and the father came and brought the sandwich. As silly as this sounded to every adult involved in this case, the father's act of atonement changed this boy's life.

Doing versus Talking

Once the therapist and the client work out what all the options for restorative justice are and how it can be done, then comes the most difficult part of all. At least, it's the most difficult part for the therapist. Therapists have been trained to talk, preferably in safe and secure environments of their own choosing and at times of their own choosing. Nothing in their training has prepared them for this phase, because it requires action.

First, as noted in the cases above, it requires at least an earnest attempt to find the abuser. This may seem impossible. But if preparatory work was done in previous phases, with the knowledge that this phase was coming sooner or later, it is often quite possible for the therapist to find the offender and, sometimes, even to offer a chance to atone, which can also provide relief to the offender. Time has passed for them, too, and many have changed even without the benefit of therapy. Young parents grow up, people stop drinking, they settle down, they often have new families, and so on. Also, some adults have even become acutely aware of their transgression and are looking for redemption. If that is the case, the process is much easier and more satisfactory for everyone. It is much easier, of course, when the abuser has already faced legal consequences or when the abuse, if admitted, will not lead to legal involvement. It is more difficult if the abuse is newly discovered and will have to be reported to the authorities. It can take the therapist quite a long time to deal with such a scenario, and restorative justice will have to be delayed until the client can deal with legal and social-service involvement. This is one of the major obstacles to this process because most of our clients are loath to involve police or caseworkers in their abuse issues before they have even been allowed to deal with them in therapy and to clarify what *they* want to happen, not what the law says must happen.

Example: When U landed at Third Way Center, she had undergone twenty hospitalizations for serious suicide attempts. Even in restrictive settings, she could not function. She was strikingly immature and childlike, demanding, and clinging even though she was 19 years old at the time. Getting to her trauma was not easy. But eventually, it became obvious that the trauma was her mother's death wish for her, whispered to her at night starting when she was 2 and lasting several years. The mother was approached calmly and sympathetically. And when she could see that the abuse had happened because of her relationship to her own mother, who had done the same to her, she was enormously relieved and admitted what she had done. The mother told all the family about what she had done, and she apologized and cried with U, but this was not enough for U. What she had felt from the abuse was a bleak sense of isolation, loneliness, and abandonment, and she wanted her mother to feel the same. She wanted her mother to go to a motel for a week and be all alone, with no cell phone, no visits. It took a lot of work with this upper-class family to get this accomplished, but it happened, and atonement took place. No more deadly suicide attempts occurred, although the road to full health was still very long and there still was box 5 to negotiate. But this bit of restorative justice made progress possible, and she felt "even" at last.

One of the most difficult situations occurs when the family wants to protect the offender. Access to the offender may then be difficult, and an alliance has to be forged with the most powerful member of that family. An attempt must be made to convince the offender and his or her protector that this need for restorative justice is present in the offender as well and that it will offer freedom from painful secrets for them, too. Sometimes, the social service system or the legal system makes this process difficult, since the fear of prosecution hangs over the family. It is not always easy to integrate all these different systems' demands in this process. It is so difficult, in fact, that it is astonishing how often therapists expect the client to do most of this work. And yet, at this point, it is the therapist who must be creative, offering possible solution scenarios to all involved in the case! It is the therapist, guided by the client, who will need to take the lead in the family meetings.

Usually, however, the justice demands of the child are very doable, even though sometimes very strange. The variety of legal, moral, ethical, and not unhealthy (i.e., not physically dangerous) ways that a child can get the feeling of *being heard,* of having imposed some sort of consequence on the perpetrator, is really infinite. It requires patient listening to the child and the adolescent, both of them present within the same person: the client. But it nearly always also requires the help and intervention, the courage, the wisdom, and the guidance of the therapist.

It is the nature of human beings to need justice. To be fully human and have the world in balance, human beings must have the restoration of balance between good and evil. The ancient Egyptians called it *ba'at,* many Chinese call it the *Tao,* and the Judeo-Christian lineages call it *atonement.* All of these require a deed, a doing, to make things right. Balance restored makes it possible to let go of old rage and the feelings of utter defeat that most of our clients suffer from. Most therapists have gone through these boxes more or less successfully in their own lives, and they have known that people who offended against them or against significant others in their lives must do penance before that relationship can be reestablished. And yet, they still find it difficult to stand by their clients in this process.

Many deeply religious Christians have the most difficulty with this aspect of trauma recovery. In a recent book, *Pope Francis: Conversations with Jorge Bergoglio,* by Francesca Ambrogetti and Sergio Rubin, the newly elected Pope Francis I was asked, "But is it possible to forgive someone who doesn't show remorse for the wrong he's committed? And who, in the words of the catechism, shows no willingness to somehow atone for the wrong he's done?" The pope said, among other things, "You can't say, 'I forgive you, and so nothing happened here.' What would have happened at the Nuremberg trials if they had adopted this attitude toward the Nazi leaders? Many atoned via execution; for others, it was prison." He also said something else that is applicable to this chapter: "If someone wrongs me, I have to forgive him, but that forgiveness is received by the other person only when he shows remorse and atones." His is certainly the way healthy adults manage wrongs done to them: judicially, legally, and wisely. Our clients need much help with this, first allowing the injured child to have his or her say. And as in the quote above, the best outcome is when the perpetrator does show remorse and is able to atone. It is best for both the abuser and the child.

In both cases cited above, the perpetrators could receive forgiveness only after actually doing some penance to demonstrate their sorrow for the injury they had inflicted on their victim. And that penance had to be done in language, imagery, and—most importantly—behavior that the victimized child could understand.

It would be fair and just if all perpetrator treatment, especially the offense-specific treatment protocol, would take this into consideration. In the "clarification" phase of that protocol, the offender has to be confronted by the victim, who gets to tell the offender how the offense has affected them. Would it not make sense if the victim were also allowed to tell the abuser what justice, what kind of atonement, would restore balance in the victim's life? It would give the abuser a specific task to complete and would allow them to feel the great gift, not only of shame over what they have done, but also of redemption and forgiveness.

You can never go home again.

To the victim, too, it often appears that "adult justice" will restore the balance of life. But, of course, it doesn't satisfy the injured child within. And just as often, the victim has the impression that once the injured child within gets justice, this will give him or her back the childhood that was lost to the trauma. Thus, the victim will tell the therapist that the justice they want is for their parent to come and play with them on the playground or go and "have fun" with them in the park. The hope and the dream is that this will restore the lost "good times" that, as the victim well knows, every child needs and deserves. But alas, it cannot be. Nothing and no one can bring back the lost times. This is true for adults, too, and should be kept in mind. When the waiter gets the order wrong, spills soup on the table, is rude and careless, and generally makes our long-anticipated dinner miserable, we want to "get even" with him. We leave two cents as a tip; we complain to the manager; we "stand up for ourselves." And by doing so, we feel better, ready to try a dinner out again. No healthy adult lets insult pile up on top of insult and then simply gives up on ever going out to dinner again. Our clients, on the other hand, have given up. But also, no healthy adult then expects ever to get that evening back. It is gone forever, and there is no retrieving it. Our clients, though, because they think about their trauma as children think of loss, *do* expect that they will have that evening back—that is, that they will have that lost time and that lost life back. And they imagine that in getting it back, they can play, laugh, and be children again. But, of course, they can't. It is the therapist's job to gently point this out and help them avoid having yet another disappointing experience.

Example: G came to Third Way Center after a long experience of neglect and abandonment by her mother. But
by the time she was a teen, her mother had "cleaned
up her act," as G said. She had quit using drugs, was
no longer homeless, and had sought G out. G was still
angry and thought it would be just and fair if her mother
parented her again and was "nice" to her. By this, she
meant that her mother should care for her physically,
which she had never done before. Mother, too, wanted
to make up for all that lost time and spent hours with
her, doing her hair, helping her with clothes, giving
her money. Meanwhile, G's behavior deteriorated with
each passing day. She finally broke down and cried
when she discovered that it was too late—the time had
come and gone, and nothing she or her mother could
do would recapture it. It was then that she had to deal
with the rage that had fueled most of her life. Only then
could she and her therapist talk about the things her
mother could do to make her hurt inner child feel that
she had "gotten even" for the loss. It took patient listening to the child, both by the therapist and the mother—
and by the client as well.

On the other hand, if atonement takes place, mother and child
sometimes do become friends and establish an adult relationship.

Example: Z had been placed with Social Services in
Massachusetts after his mother had neglected him and
was reported to the police. She was a teen mother without support. Over the next several years, Z was moved
from foster home to foster home. Because he also suf-

fered from severe ADHD, he acted out in school and in placements and was therefore constantly moved. Eventually, he landed in a treatment facility in Utah, then in South Carolina, and, finally, in Colorado. Because he didn't "get better" but became increasing destructive, he came to Third Way Center. By then, he had lost all contact with family. Nobody seemed to know where they were. It took a year to help him. He got on the right medication worked through the boxes to box 4. At that point, we needed to find the family. This took sifting through boxes and boxes of records, writing letters to various state social service agencies, and contacting past placements, but eventually, his mother was discovered in Montgomery, Alabama. When we contacted her, she was overjoyed. She had grown up on her own, without even Social Services to help, and was now married to an auto mechanic and had two small children. But she had never forgotten Z. Z was about to graduate from Joan Farley Academy at Third Way Center. The mother immediately volunteered to come and attend his graduation, because I told her straightaway, as he had instructed me, that if things were ever to be okay, she had to come to him this time. We offered her an airline ticket. She refused, saying she needed to pay for this herself and that it was a gift to him from her. Coming to Denver took her fifty-one hours by Greyhound Bus. She stayed only a day. But she had atoned. Z knew this and was delighted. After graduation, he stayed in contact with her and got to know his stepfather. His stepfather eventually got him a job in Alabama, and Z moved into the apartment building where his family was living. A relationship formed, and though he never recaptured his lost childhood, he moved into a productive, rage-free adult relationship with his mother and his new family.

Existential Traumas

Other traumas, too, have severely derailed clients' lives—traumas for which the answer to "What is justice?" is harder to find. The trauma of having a severe biological illness or physically disabling trauma is hard to manage for most teens. It often results not only in severely incapacitating bad behavior but also in patients who are recalcitrant and uncooperative with the doctors trying to help them. Children with severe brittle diabetes are a good example of this. Most of these children's parents feel as guilty as if they had willingly perpetrated this unjust trauma on them. And the disease or disability causes just as much acting out and havoc in the family as do acts that are more traditionally thought of as trauma.

The process of the six boxes can be applied to these clients, also. When arriving at box 4, however, it is clear that for most of these clients and their families, restorative justice becomes an existential issue. *Why me? What is the purpose of my suffering?* These become the issues of justice. Adolescence is an opportune time to address this since these are questions that most normal adolescents also ask and have to answer. Spiritual help and advice, data collected in the "Spiritual and Cultural" bin, should be put to use. The great author and psychiatrist Viktor Frankl has addressed this issue in his work on existential psychotherapy. It will be useful to refer to his work.

> **Example:** When G arrived at Third Way Center, one arm had been amputated after being severely mauled by a dog. Though he strongly professed to be "just

fine," he was a very angry, hostile, acting-out young man. The mauling had occurred after his mother left him in the care of a very young babysitter. The mother gave permission for his arm to be amputated. While in therapy, G did get down to box 3 and was able to talk about his rage at his mother and his wish to punish her by his acting out. He blamed her fiercely for his misfortune. Unfortunately, neither he nor his mother resolved this while in treatment. They both loved each other deeply, and both agreed—in words, anyway—that the accident was an act of fate. In retrospect, it would have been much more helpful to involve her pastor from the beginning because, for both of them, this trauma involved the seriously existential issue of "Why me?" and "Why would God let such a thing happen?"

This form of severe trauma—the trauma with no real perpetrator—is the most difficult both to address and to resolve and requires even greater action and inventiveness from the therapist. Getting justice from God or fate or genetics is difficult and requires much sublimation and great spiritual healing on the part of both the client and the family. Still, it is possible to apply the same strategies, and this has been done successfully with a number of severely diabetic teens.

Example: J came to Third Way Center because she was a diabetic young woman who had been unable and unwilling to follow a diabetic regimen, which would have controlled her severely fluctuating blood glucose levels. She was angry and resentful because her diabetes had prevented her from participating in school activities without the constraint of always having to measure her blood sugar level and take shots of insulin, which made her feel defective and worth less than her "normal" teen friends. She was furious with God for saddling her with this disability and was deeply offensive to her very religious parents. She really needed to answer the question "Why me?" When another diabetic adolescent came to the unit, J discovered that she had a great ability to counsel the new arrival. Gradually, she understood that perhaps her diabetes would allow her to be of great help to others.

Despite the client's and the therapist's deep fears when entering this stage of trauma resolution, the joy of actually being able to *do* something about the injuries inflicted brings with it greater self-esteem and, usually, a psychological growth spurt. As with brain development, activating the left-sided limbic system and then moving data from the affect-perceiving right prefrontal cortex to the left prefrontal cortex moves the person toward maturity and better control both behaviorally and emotionally. This is a good index for the therapist to gauge whether the therapy has been for the correct trauma and whether the justice has been the right justice for that particular injury in that particular client. As they say, the proof is in the pudding!

BOX 5.

New Feelings

Stage I

Most people, including the client, will expect that once the restorative justice piece has been accomplished, they will feel miraculously cured. But, of course, the aftereffects of getting justice are not always precisely what the client or the treatment team expected. Still, to verify that the process was correct, there must be a discernible decrease in acting out.

There also should be, initially, a great sense of relief, of triumph. This is an important indicator that some sense of justice for the injured child has been achieved. If this feeling of success, of winning, is not present, the therapist needs to consider that the client may have chosen the particular act of restorative justice for all the wrong reasons. The client may have heard or seen a peer do this, and that peer found satisfaction. Or it may be that the therapist suggested some action that seemed to the therapist safe and appropriate. Or it may be that both client and therapist are working on the wrong trauma. Most often, though, it is the therapist's lack of patience and lack of empathic support that get in the way of the child's speaking up. Most commonly, the adolescent client is embarrassed and feels that it's "childish" to tell the adult therapist what the restorative act might be. Therefore, this is the stage that will, by the affect exhibited by the client, prove whether box 4 was accomplished.

It is important to see a sense of pride in having had the courage to stand up and be heard, to have "shown them." There is pride in being fully human and having restored some balance. This contributes much to the client's new self-esteem over moving away from the idea of being the eternal victim. It also helps the client give up the thought that there are only two kinds of human beings: victims and perpetrators. When clients first come to Third Way Center, they universally believe that it is an eat-or-be-eaten world. Getting real justice does much to change that worldview. It makes the clients think that they can, in fact, be heard and understood and can defend themselves appropriately—and, best of all, to the benefit of everyone!

For example, H, the young man who peed on his father's grave, felt elated and thoroughly justified. He felt that he had been able to express to his father how the abuse had made him feel small and hopeless. The young woman who first taught me about the need for justice told me that the justice she wanted was to be heard by the people who trusted her father. After confronting them, she felt elated and empowered. She told me that she felt "grown up." The young man who had demanded the sandwich from his father joyfully ate it, telling everyone about how his father had recognized his childhood hunger and atoned for it. The young woman who had her mother spend the week alone in the motel was all grins. Interestingly, though, she had empathy with her mother because the mother now "really knew" how she had felt as a young child: unwanted and isolated.

That feeling of having achieved some long-desired goal is one of the hallmarks of knowing whether the restorative justice really was correct for a particular client. If that feeling is not present, then no matter what the adolescent says, it was not right for the child victim. It will take effort then to go back even to the very beginning, to bin 1 if necessary. This is tremendously hard for nearly any therapist. It involves accepting that however hard the therapist tried, however understanding, kind, empathic, and clever the therapist thought they were being, they got it wrong! It means having to go back to bin 1 and reviewing all the available old data, looking at it with fresh eyes and with the client. It means finding what the missing pieces might be, where missing history is hiding. It requires true persistence and dedication to the client. Whenever that happens, as disastrous as it might seem to the therapist, the effect on the client can be nothing short of amazing. Instead of giving up, the client is usually astonished (a) that a therapist would ever admit to being wrong; (b) that, for a change, it might not all be the client's fault; and (c) that someone would stick with them no matter how long and difficult the journey to healing their trauma. So however traumatic this might be for the therapist, and however angry it makes the outside treatment team, it always seems to result in a much more solid alliance with the client.

> **Example:** T had told of some serious abuse inflicted early in life by her father. She had heard about the boy who peed on his father's grave, and she thought she wanted to do the same. So she took some urine to her father's grave and poured it on. She felt silly, and it clearly was not her particular justice. But she had to find this out on her own! Her justice had nothing to do with this act, which was neither age nor gender appropriate. As a matter of fact, on going back to history and the meanings of the first two boxes, it turned out that the abuser was not the father at all but the female babysitter, at a much earlier age, and the justice had nothing whatever to do with peeing on anyone's grave.

There are no shortcuts. There is only the patience of listening. And not just patience on the part of the therapist, but also patience and empathy and compassion on the part of the teen client toward the victim child within. If the justice was not correct for the child, it might mean going back only to box 2: the feelings underlying the behavior that the client needs to have empathy with. Or, as noted above, it may need a reevaluation of just what the original trauma really was.

Stage II
But even if the restorative justice was the right one for the particular client, more often than not, after the elation the client feels a sense of loss that comes with the end of the conflict.

At the end of box 4, there often comes a sense of what the client missed through the abuse—the loss of a great part of childhood and, often, the loss of the family they wish they had had. Thus, sadness and mourning frequently come in the wake of restorative justice and its initial sense of triumph. But now mourning is possible. If the client is prepared for this, it is the final step in letting go of the past and itself becomes a healing process. Often, the fantasy is that once justice is restored, reconciliation with the abuser will come about. But even if the abuser participated and did penance, a relationship such as should have existed between the adult and the child really never comes to pass. The time for that has come and gone, and at best, there is a standoff, with new rules and new problems. There is still the issue that they have been robbed of a part of their childhood and, therefore, have developmental delays that must be addressed both in therapy and in real life. Still, this is the point where growth and growing up can begin.

Take, for example, U, whose mother had whispered death wishes to her and later apologized and atoned. U could accept that she and her mother would never have the relationship that both now wished they had had. Together, they mourned that loss. They accepted that it could never be, that it was too late. But U had major difficulties mourning the loss of her childhood and the missed opportunities to practice growing up. After all the hard work she had done to get justice, she wanted to be "done," to automatically acquire all the skills of young adulthood. Dating, rejection, and friendships all seemed overwhelming to her, and she longed to be her "sick" old suicidal self.

H, the young man who peed on his father's grave, was able to grieve thoroughly, and now he enthusiastically wanted to practice being a young college student. Another example was the young woman whose mother had rejected her early, choosing alcohol and drugs instead of her. But she, the daughter, had always believed that she had been a "bad girl" and that this was why her mother had rejected her. And she had certainly tried to prove that she was "bad" and unlovable. She wanted to go and find her mother. And find her we did, in Alabama. We took a trip with the daughter, and her mother refused to see her face to face, though the daughter caught a glimpse of her as she tried to avoid contact. She heard her mother cry behind the slammed door, and it vindicated her. But her stepfather did see her, and her grandmother talked with her, too. The grandmother and the stepfather explained the mother's alcoholism and her shame. And the young woman, too, cried at her mother's door. Going there gave her closure and a sense of loss but also the recognition that it was not her being "bad" that had made the mother reject her. And she had been vindicated by her grandmother and her stepfather. It made her deeply sad, but it freed her from the tremendous guilt of having felt all her life that she deserved the abandonment by her mother.

Stage III

This last example brings up the most problematic aspect of this phase: the issue of identity. For years, the trauma has been the single organizing principle in the client's life. Actions, thoughts, feelings, and relationships have all been colored and determined to a large extent by the abuse, by the trauma. Trauma had shaped the client's identity as a less than whole person. And this identity had shaped the client's behavior, attachments, and relationships. But more than that, this trauma-sculpted identity had taken center stage, consuming and directing much of the psychic energy that the client expended and concentrated on. It also had become familiar. In some strange way, it was comfortable territory, predictable and known. It knew what was to be expected, and everything always turned out just as the client had known it would. People and actions had assigned places. Also, this identity provided a great deal of energy and excitement while distracting the client from other developmental tasks. Our clients are adolescents, and adolescents already crave stimulation. Thus, when the overstimulation of the sympathomimetic system that happens with trauma gets added to the mix, the sudden peace and lack of uproar (after the restorative justice, when the trauma is no longer center stage) is perceived as painful, restless, and uncomfortable.

The important thing at this point is to help the client mourn the loss of certainty of feelings and behavior that trauma gives, and to be empathic with the client's sense of being at sea and feeling a bit empty. But the therapist must also help the client prepare for the issues that every adolescent has to address: identity and separation. Some clients, glad to be freed, take eagerly to this, but for most, it's hard. For the old preoccupations no longer apply, and giving up one's distress is as difficult as giving up any other familiar thing, good, bad, or indifferent. A loss is a loss is a loss. And adolescent nature abhors a vacuum. Thus, the therapist at this point needs to lend the client a lot of support as a mentor in the process of forging a new identity. Experimentation with one's identity and forming new relationships eventually take the place of the previous preoccupations with the abuse. They thus become the entrée into box 6: new behavior.

For example, both U, whose mother whispered death wishes to her, and H, who peed on his father's grave, changed appearances, experimented with who they were, and started relationships outside their usual circle. Both started college. Both, relatively late in an adolescent's usual life cycle, started to date, often struggling with issues that 13- and 14-year-olds struggle with, even though both were 20 at the time. Sexuality and attachment issues vied with each other in an often typically adolescent fashion, confusing them, their therapists, and their families.

Stage IV
If the family, too, has made a lot of progress by this point, it is the family who will then take over this part of the client's growth, and that is the preferable outcome. But still a little more work has to be done in family therapy before this can happen. A lot of affect will be stirred up in the family. Even ordinary adolescents are baffling and disruptive to most families. How much more so these newly minted ones who, chronologically, should be much further along in that process. Families respond with varying degrees of support to the restorative justice sought by the client. Also, they, like the client, are just getting over that part in the healing process. They feel anxious and unsure whether this process might be right and how much trouble it is apt to cause the family. Often, family members feel cheated. After they themselves never got justice, how was it possible for this young member of their family to find it! Sometimes, a bit of envy is wrapped up in the package. And sometimes, that can lead to their own need for justice, and they ask for the six boxes. All this has to be addressed continuously in family therapy.

If all went well, then other family members also either went through, or want to go through, the process of healing their own trauma via the six boxes And they, too, may have found their justice or may yet find it. A new and healthier family unit will emerge. Sometimes, though, the family has been deeply divided by this process, and it will be difficult for the client not to accept responsibility for that. The family might blame the client for the upheaval that the process of justice has caused. Some may not ever forgive the client, but if the family has been part of the ongoing process, they, too, have had a say in whether the atonement the client sought was appropriate. Clients and families may need a great deal of supportive and ongoing psychotherapy.

As an example of this, U's stepfather was puzzled and angry with U for demanding that her mother atone, since he felt that U had cost the family untold hours of tragedy and no end of money, which should certainly count toward atonement. It took a lot of work for him to see that previous therapies had tried to show U that all the trouble she caused was "restorative justice" enough, and that these attempts had not worked. Indeed, they had only escalated the pressure that the child victim brought on U. He was also afraid for his wife in that motel room—afraid of having no contact with her. He allowed it only after much discussion and built-in safeguards. But after he began to see U "grow up"—function better, cease her severely self-destructive behavior—he became supportive. But he had hoped, nay, *expected* that everything would be fine once she gave up her suicidality. He quickly forgot how grateful he and the family were for that. As U struggled with her adolescent behavior, her push-pull with independence versus dependence, he once again remembered all the trouble she had caused the family. But he could resolve this in therapy and actually began to form a fairly healthy father-daughter relationship with her, getting involved with her around her car, her money management, and so on.

It is not unusual for the family, the client manager, the caseworker, or even the therapist—in other words, any or all of the team around the client—to feel this way, namely that the client's severe acting out has punished the world sufficiently and it should now be over. And that is the whole point: the *world* was punished, not the abuser!

Therefore, at this stage, it may be helpful to go back and have the client return to a dialectical behavior therapy group to once again manage the strong feelings and remind the client of the principles of self-soothing and awareness. In addition, a brief period of psychopharmacology with antianxiety medication may be helpful to the client. The family, too, may need to be taught DBT principles and supportive therapy so they can tolerate the wide range of affect seen in this box.

The entire gamut of problems that come with growing up will take center stage next, and a new set of behaviors emerges. The family, too, may need to seek outpatient therapy, just as many parents of even "normal" adolescents do.

BOX 6.

New Behavior

As THIS MANUAL has progressed, it should have become clear that the entire process is very *fluid*. This means that throughout the six boxes, the client often returns to well-used and all-too-familiar patterns of behavior and feelings. At least, there often is a curiously nostalgic wish for the secondary gains, the perks, of the traumatized child. Also, old, well-used techniques of dealing with problems and obstacles—no matter how unhelpful or even downright dysfunctional, painful, and unsuccessful these methods have proved to be—are at least familiar and well practiced. They are predictable, and there is always the hope that this time, the usual flawed and discredited way of dealing with the world will be successful and bring peace. Add the fact that most of our clients have not had many opportunities to practice and try out a wide variety of different techniques for handling life's challenges and obstacles, and their fear for the future is understandable.

The "New" Adolescent

But also, fortunately, besides the traumatized child whom the previous steps, or boxes, have dealt with, there is also an adolescent on board, and that adolescent can mourn the past and experiment with new behavior. Unfortunately, that requires a lot of therapy and teaching.

> **Example:** W had come to Third Way Center at 17 with the usual extensive history of abuse in early childhood and then an extensive string of failed placements, resulting in much abandonment and neglect. With a lot of therapeutic effort, he went through the first four boxes, even arriving with happily at box 5. But then the reality of all the developmental delays that his trauma had caused him set in. His first relationship with a girl proved sadly disappointing because of his immature demands. He had never practiced having relationships before, and now he was 18 and "should know better." He went back to dealing with his anger by smoking THC. After all, getting high had kept him from feeling his feelings before. But he had a relationship with his family and his therapist now, and he could talk to them about it. Also, as he said, getting high wasn't so much fun anymore. He went back to box 1 but found it less useful. He had grown up a bit without knowing it.

Normal Ways to Handle Trauma

However much the client struggles, the new behaviors that emerge are healthier and more productive. But above all, the client has learned a technique for handling trauma that, to most people, seems second nature. The thought that trauma, even minor insults, must be addressed—and, preferably, to the person who inflicted the trauma—is second nature to most people. There may be many factors that prevent a person from being able to respond immediately or as directly as they would like. But that then takes a toll. Much thought, rumination, sharing with friends about what might have been done or said, goes on! This often draws a lot of psychic energy away from developmental tasks, and it can be repeated only so many times before injury upon injury piles up and preoccupies the person, to the exclusion of normal tasks. All people have known "martyrs" in their lives—people who pile injury upon injury, never resolving matters to satisfaction.

This, multiplied by a thousand, is the trauma of our clients. And thus, the restorative justice must also be multiplied by a thousand, since the trauma has robbed them of whole swaths of developmental task completion. The therapist or, preferably, the family must now deal with the developmental deficits and help the client recapture those particular missed skills.

It is interesting to note that since all nature pushes toward equilibrium and since adolescents, in all their chaos, particularly long for equilibrium, they seem eager to learn these skills—not always gracefully, but always enthusiastically. At this point, it is best to go with what nature has decreed, namely that children, if not seriously interfered with, will grow up and want to master skills of adulthood, provided that they are freed of the bonds of their trauma.

For example, U might still be annoying with her calls and her occasional temper outbursts, but she is no longer swallowing razor blades or jumping off buildings. Her concerns are dating, her car, and her college dorm room. There are times when she gets nostalgic for the attention and care she received while she was considered "so sick." At first, she often wished she were getting the fire department to come and take her to the hospital again, as it used to. But those wistful thoughts have become less and less frequent. As she grieved the loss of her childhood and the loss of the mother she wished she had had, she became freer to explore other areas of her life. As a matter of fact, she and her mother began to know each other as adults, and mostly they like each other— like each other enough even to be able to spend a vacation together. U, like nearly everyone else, faces a future with hope. There will be other tragedies in her life. Nobody promised her a rose garden, as the saying goes, but she will become stronger because of what she has survived, and she should be proud.

Mopping Up

Most of our clients have left Third Way Center by this phase. Maybe they have also been able to practice the entire process through the smaller traumas, trials, and tribulations that life in a psychiatric treatment center brings. Living with many other unhappy, angry, traumatized young people certainly provides many opportunities both to practice the six boxes and to help others do the same. The schematic of the boxes is written and rewritten by each client with their particular behavior, with the particular feelings that drive their behavior, with their particular trauma, with their particular restorative justice, with their particular feelings that this engenders, and, ultimately, with their particular new behavior, leading to whatever life they choose.

It is noteworthy that throughout this process of seeking justice that restores balance, nearly every kind of therapy, from psychoanalytical formulation to cognitive behavioral therapy, to DBT, to psychotherapy, to psychopharmacology, has been employed. And yet, the schema—the drawing of the boxes—is understandable and helpful, even for clients with relatively low IQs, and it is doable for clients who have almost no ability to form concepts. The basic need for justice transcends these handicaps. It exists in us all, regardless of how smart or not smart we are and regardless of what the trauma is.

As we noted in boxes 3 and 4, it may seem that the therapist and the client have gone through all the steps, ticking them off one by one until they appear to have landed, in no time, in box 6. And the therapist is understandably elated to believe that justice was done for the adolescent. And yet, the client returns to acting out severely with self-destructive behaviors. As discouraging as that may feel to both, there are only two possible answers: (1) the trauma worked on was not the driving force in the client's life; or, much more commonly, (2) the "justice" that the therapist and client had decided on was not sufficient or was too adult. It may have been appropriate for an adult or an adolescent but inappropriate (and impossible) for the child who had been injured by the abuse.

Therefore, again, much to the therapist's dismay, the situation requires going back to step one. At this point, it helps to reread *all* the notes between the therapist and the client, reread *all* the past treatment history, and reexamine the six history bins to see what was missed. It requires the therapist to be able to wipe the slate clean and let go of any sense of failure and hurt pride. Rarely does the client object. It is as if they had known all along, throughout the treatment process, that the wrong tack was taken. If anything, they are impressed by the therapist's ability to admit mistakes. They admire the persistence and take hope from it. This second look uses hindsight in a most constructive way and has a better chance of being right—provided, of course, that the therapist can look at the case a second time, freed of prejudice and the need to be right. Even if this process has to be repeated three or four times, it will eventually become clear to both therapist and client what is *the* restorative justice that is "enough," that satisfies the child victim.

> **Example:** As mentioned in the discussion on taking histories, a client had been to Third Way Center twice and had been "treated" for months with grief therapy over his mother's supposed suicide. Despite devoted care, he didn't get any better. As a matter of fact, he only increased his raging and angry behavior, making it more and more difficult to tolerate him, let alone be empathic. And that is the salient point: he didn't get

better; he got worse. There was only one thing to do: go back and redo the entire process. And the second time, a new answer to his distress emerged, namely that he felt responsible for her suicide. Moreover, it turned out most likely not to have been a suicide at all, but a case of accidental death from substance abuse. This did change his affect and his behavior and required an entirely new look at what justice was for him. When this was done, this time his affect was "right." As I watched him come bounding into the center with a grin on his face, talking away, I asked him how he felt. He stopped and said, "Hopeful. I feel hopeful." Is there a better start to a new life?

Another example is K, who had been to Third Way Center on two previous occasions. Each time, she seemed to have worked through her trauma, was pleasant and grateful, and always fell back to her previous behavior. On rethinking her case, it turned out that she had been so protective of her therapist that she could not tell him about the sexual abuse she received from her beloved parents, though she had hinted at it often enough in histories taken and retaken! Only the third time around, when her therapist admitted his failure to address her trauma and deal with her parents even though their rights had been terminated, could she trust him. And this time around, she finished her trauma work.

Time constraints, money shortages, failure to conceptualize a case correctly—all have resulted in a lot of our clients being unable to complete this process or, sometimes, even to get started in it. Sometimes, it has been possible only to teach a client the steps and have them observe the steps in their infinite variety as their peers are going through them. But it is the apparent simplicity of the boxes that they remember most.

A New Life

Throughout the forty-four or so years of Third Way Center's history, it has been our great good fortune to have clients come back to see us, or write us letters about how they managed to remember and use this process. Their lives have not been all smooth, either, but they have managed to stay employed and to avoid reincarceration. The ones who have been sex offenders have not reoffended and, thus, have not created more victims. They have not all gone to college and become rich—the six boxes have not solved the problems of poverty and biological handicaps. But the six boxes have allowed our clients to choose their own future and learn to deal with whatever else life had in store for them. This is good not only for the client but also for society at large. It saves untold money for the state and the country and produces productive members of society. And it prevents unimaginable grief and further suffering.

Afterword

MUCH OF THE MATERIAL in this manual just constitutes the principles of good practice. There have, however, been many attempts at
"therapeutic shortcuts," through various "brief" interventions that
center only on eliminating specific problematic behaviors or feelings.
They all skip the step of spending valuable time and effort on taking
a history or even getting to know the client. Others have tried to discover a one-size-fits-all, often totally rote approach to psychotherapy,
without regard to an individual client's needs or circumstances. Perhaps, this came about partly in response to the inordinate amount of
time required by the psychoanalytic approach, in which only the client
determined the course of therapy. Eventually, each of these therapeutic
approaches probably helped some clients figure out how to deal with
their trauma. But in reality, all victims have had to find their own way
of trauma resolution, and each resolution had to fit a specific trauma
inflicted on a specific client. It's hard work, a client at a time.

But over the past two decades, psychiatric treatment for children
and adolescents has become harder and harder to come by as inpatient units either disappeared or became "stabilization units"—places
where a few days of respite and a medication adjustment are deemed

sufficient treatment. The assumption is that the child or adolescent
should then be able to resume a normal life, with no real thought to
whether the client is up to the task. Trauma is never really mentioned
or even asked about! After all, treatment is about "stabilization," whatever that may mean. Psychiatric outpatient therapy has virtually disappeared. Psychiatric treatment for 18- to 21-year-olds, unless they have
private funding, is all but nonexistent. And because most traumatized
adolescents are angry and hostile toward the world around them, they
commit a great number of crimes. So they get incarcerated a lot. They
become criminals and cost the taxpayers a lot of money.

So the jails have filled with more and more adolescents. But to be
fair, it became apparent to the authorities that a great number of incarcerated children had suffered severe childhood trauma and were acting
out some injury specific to them. It was really impossible in a system
designed for punishment, that is, a jail, to establish a system where
that specificity of trauma could be adequately addressed. But what was
clear was that the subjects' anger seemed to be nonspecifically acted
out on anyone and everyone. One thing was certain: they were angry!
Their anger was very often uncontrollable, and manifested in the form
of their having become vicious predators. And then they had to pay for
their angry acting out and, it was hoped, taught a lesson that would
prevent them from becoming criminals and acting out forever. The
juvenile justice system came up with the term "restorative justice." It's
a great term and very apt.

To be fair, the juvenile justice system also recognized that many
of its inmates were indeed traumatized, and it began to concentrate
on that trauma. And so the term "trauma-informed therapy" came to
be. Their staff and ours went to a multitude of seminars on this topic.
What people learned was that all actions by the incarcerated youths
who had been victimized were colored and formed by the trauma they
had undergone. Therefore, in talking with them, this should become

the focal issue and they should learn to "deal" with this trauma. And they should resolve it by various therapeutic models such as DBT, which became all the rage, and, when that did not seem quite satisfactory, by other methods such as cognitive behavioral therapy, REM therapy, breathing exercises, and so on. Everyone was really looking to help those teens—and, preferably, by a method that could be applied in a very standardized, replicable method. We are still looking for that, but at least we really do seem to know that childhood abuse, or trauma, causes vast harm.

But nowhere did any of the new wisdom say what the therapist or the client can *do* about the trauma except always to take it into consideration when dealing with a client. And nobody had thought to ask our clients what *they wanted to do* about their trauma. I had only asked my client out of sheer frustration and, yes, boredom. I think almost everyone is afraid to ask a juvenile, especially a delinquent juvenile, what they might want to do to their abusers. The thought is that it would be something horrific and totally illegal. It took me a long time to figure out that it was not the adolescent or even the adult who would answer, but the child who had been abused. In retrospect, that was easy to see. These two discoveries were the basis of the Six Boxes to Trauma Recovery. Indeed, they were the two basic principles of the process:

- Trauma requires justice, fairness, which must be restored by the abuser through his or her penance.
- That justice always takes place within the developmental phase during which the trauma was inflicted, and is determined solely by the victim *at that stage.*

One more discovery remained to be made: this particular developmental phase, namely adolescence, was the easiest time to be in touch with that child. Psychotherapists had long known that adolescence is God's or nature's second chance to fix developmental issues that went wrong in childhood. As ego dissolution occurs with the onset of puberty, much material that had been unconscious during latency or early childhood becomes available to conscious thought. An adolescent can, for the first time, think about thinking and think about how it should have been, what might have been, and what actually was. This new awareness brings with it all the affective material stored and buried in childhood, and it demands action.

Thus, it is in this particular stage of development when we are most in touch with our own unconscious, with long-forgotten wishes, thoughts, and possible actions. So it makes sense that the stage during which a developmental arrest occurred should become available to the conscious mind. It becomes evident to the client, too, that development stopped at way too early a stage—and that it stopped for a specific reason. Adolescents get infuriated when someone points out their developmental deficits, but in calmer moments, they admit that they are sorely lacking in those skills.

The deficits are particularly and poignantly obvious when the abuse was sexual in nature. A client (quoted earlier) said it perfectly in a group. When asked, "Why is sexual abuse of children wrong?" he alone knew the answer. He said, "Because ever after that, I thought only of sex when I should have learned to play!" No play, no learning and practicing growing up. He was talking about all the opportunities he had missed to learn to become an adult. That is, after all the developmental tasks of childhood, we are practicing growing up. Adult life is about so much more than sex. That was what he was so sad about. And he was terribly angry despite loving his abuser and having liked the sex. He had to learn to take back all that energy he had invested in the abuse and the abuser. What U, the young woman with the death-whispering mother, had cathected—spent all her psychic energy on— was the trauma. The act of getting justice takes that back; it allows the client to decathect, to disconnect their psychic energy from it.

The lucky thing is that our clients at Third Way Center are adolescents, and at no other time in a human being's development is the push toward growth stronger. Adolescents really do want to grow up. They are chomping at the bit to do so. They, more than any other group of people, absolutely hate being "sick" or "handicapped," especially by their own past. It's a bit of a double-edged sword because they are also better than any child or adult at denying any and all handicaps. But given the amount of trouble our clients are in and given the spectacular lack of success they have had doing it "their way," they are also easier to convince that there is another way for them to be free.

Convincing adolescents that freedom comes with resolution can be difficult, but milieu therapy lends itself uniquely to the task. That's because being there at the very moment when their action gets them in trouble again provides the ideal opportunity to be in the moment with observations of behavior and feelings. Adolescents have notoriously bad memories for unpleasant events that involve bad actions on their part. In residential care, as luck would have it, there's an entire squad of other adolescents alert and eager to remember another's bad behavior and only too glad to point it out. And often, it seems easier to accept that feedback from a peer than from an adult. Coming from a peer, it also often elicits more honesty about feelings.

Engaging in this process is even more difficult for adults than for adolescents. A great many of our clients' parents, grandparents, step-parents, or other older family members also have suffered significant trauma. Abuse is often present for generations in a family. Occasionally, these adults, too, may want to do trauma-informed therapy, and some have found the six boxes wonderfully revealing and helpful. The process has given them hope of recovering themselves. Over a lifetime, it becomes increasingly harder to listen to what the traumatized child within wants, and adults have more difficulty even than adolescents in giving up their attachment to doing what they have always done.

One more suggestion may be helpful. It's best not to deconstruct or rearrange the boxes or turn them upside down. The steps are not really boxes. They are stages—fluid and with only the most tenuous boundaries. They allow for a lot of regression, and they are rarely if ever completed in tidy order, one after the other, no matter how fervently both adolescent and therapist wish it were so. The steps are inextricably linked to each other. So if deconstructed and taken one by one, they are reduced to mere disconnected exercises with no unifying structure, rather than a complete holistic process. Moreover, trying to use them separately doesn't allow for the ebb and flow of progress.

Also, this may seem to therapists to be an uphill process, so the temptation is to put "old behavior" on the bottom and make "new behavior" the first box on top. But all teaching of the written word in school starts at the top and goes downward, so an adolescent school-age child will automatically go from top to bottom. It is much harder for them to start from the bottom and work upward than to go from the top down. It's already an uphill struggle for them, and we don't need to compound the difficulty. Their eyes are fixed on step one, and in all their experience, step one of any process starts at the top, not at the bottom.

Adolescents also often will try to embellish the six boxes with a lot of artwork until there is no room to write in the boxes. But the boxes are not canvases for the budding artist. Doodled flowers, curlicues, and fancy colorful backgrounds are distractions that help avoid the topic of each box. The boxes are best left unadorned and as simple as possible, leaving lots of room to write each adolescent's thoughts and observations.

Still, even though we and our clients have muddled through all the individual interpretations of the six boxes, we have had great success with this model of treating traumatized adolescents and their families. We have watched them grow and have helped them free themselves from an endless cycle of expensive, unprofitable acting out. And we have provided them with a tool they can use anytime to deal with future trauma.

Appendix

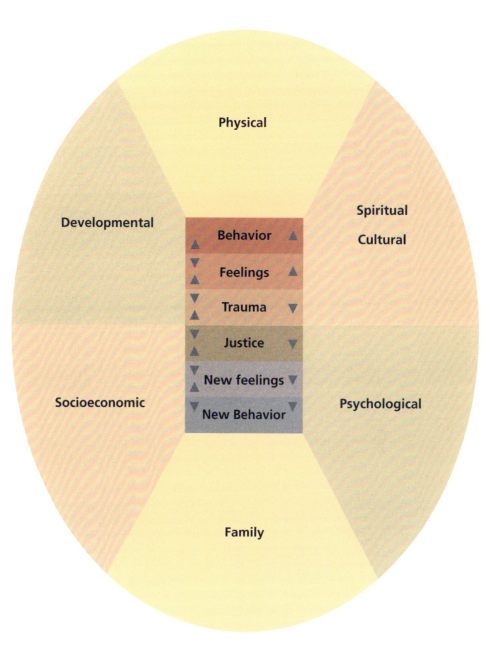

Appendix I: Model of the "Avocado"

Physical
1. Appearance
2. Function
3. Illness
4. Somatization

Developmental
1. Trust vs. Mistrust
2. Autonomy vs. Shame
3. Initiative vs. Guilt
4. Industriousness vs. Inferiority
5. Idenity vs. Role Confusion
Plus three stages of adulthood

Spiritual Cultural
1. Spiritual
   a. Religion
   b. Conscience
   c. Values
   d. Discipline
2. Culture

6 BOX MODEL

Socioeconomic
1. The Social Person
   a. Friends
   b. Socializing
   c. Sex
   d. Discipline
2. Economics
   a. Income & Occupation
   b. Housing

Psychological
1. Psych Testing & MS
2. IQ
3. Ego Function
   a. Concept Formation
   b. Defense Mechanisms
   c. Reality Testing

Family
1. Genogram
2. Family Function
   a. Nuclear Family
   b. Extended Family

Appendix II a: Model of the Avocado for Taking the History, with the Six Bins Enlarged

.

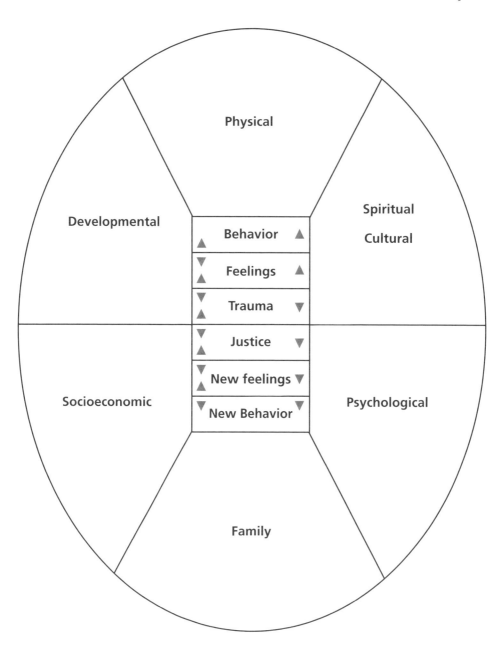

Appendix II b: Worksheet for the Avocado

Appendix III a: Model of the Avocado for Trauma Work, with the Six Boxes Enlarged

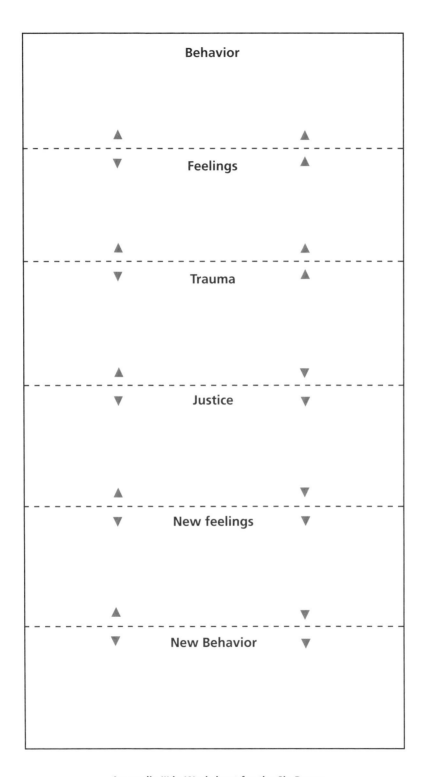

Appendix III b: Worksheet for the Six Boxes

Mental Status Exam

Client: _____

Date: _____

1. Brain Function

Orientation

Ask Date: _____

Ask Name: _____

Ask Place: _____

Organicity

Show the sequence of shapes to the client and ask client to draw the sequence on a separate sheet of paper (attached).

△ □ ◇ • • • • • • •

Fund of Knowledge

1. Who is the president of the U.S.?
2. Who do you live with?
3. Who am I?
4. What is the capital of Colorado?
5. Who is the governor of Colorado?
6. Who is the mayor of Denver?
7. What is a barometer?
8. How far is it from NY to Chicago?
9. What is the capital of Greece?
10. How many days are in a week?

11. Name the four seasons.

12. Why do we celebrate the 4th of July?

13. How many pounds are in a ton?

14. Why does oil float on water?

15. What is a prime number?

16. Who invented the airplane?

17. Where does the sun set?

2. ABILITY TO FORM CATEGORIES AND DECODE

Content of Thought

Similarities

What do these things have in common?

1. peach/plum

2. cat/mouse

3. piano/violin

4. paper/coal

5. mountain/lake

6. first/last

7. 49/121

Proverbs

1. Don't cry over spilt milk.

2. Don't count your chickens until all the eggs are hatched.

3. Don't cross your bridge until you come to them.

4. Don't burn your bridges behind you.

5. When the cats away, the mice will play.

6. The tongue is the enemy of the neck.

7. The rolling stone gathers no moss.

8. To fiddle while Rome burns.

3. ADD AND DISTRACTIBILITY

Attention & Concentration

(Have the client calculate all the way back from 100 to 1, as close as possible)

1. Serial 7's   107 100 93 86 79 72 65 58 51 44 37
30 23 16 9 2

   Serial 3's   103 100 97 94 91 88 85 82 79 76
73 70 67 64 61 58 55 52 49 46 43 40
37 34 31 28 25 22 19 16 13 10 7 4 1

Count backwards from 100

100 99 98 97 96 95 94 93 92 91 90 89 88 87 86 85
84 83 82 81 80 79 78 77 76 75 74 73 72 71 70 69 68
67 66 65 64 63 62 61 60 59 58 57 56 55 54 53 52 51 50
49 48 47 46 45 44 43 42 41 40 39 38 37 36 35 34 33 32
31 30 29 28 27 26 25 24 23 22 21 20 19 18 17 16 15 14
13 12 11 10 9 8 7 6 5 4 3 2 1

2. Digits Forward

3,8,6   6,1,2   3,4,1,7   6,1,5,8   8,4,2,3,9
5,2,1,8,6   7,9,6,4,8,3   1,6,4,5,9,7,6,3

   Backward

2,5   6,3   5,7,4   2,5,9   7,2,9,6 8,4,1,3
4,1,6,2,7   1,6,5,2,9,8   8,5,9,2,3,4,2

4. MEMORY

Recent
1. What did you eat for dinner last night?
2. When did you arrive here?
3. What is your home address?
4. What is your home phone number?

Past
1. What is your earliest memory?
2. Where did you attend elementary school?
3. What is the hospital you were born in?

Three Minute Memory
1. Ball, tennis shoe, fire hydrant

5. CONSCIENCE AND IMPULSIVITY

Judgment:
1. What would you do if you saw a fire in a movie theatre?
2. Why are criminals locked up?
3. Why should people return library books?
4. If you find a letter on the street and it is addressed and stamped, what would you do with it?

6. LETHALITY REVIEW:
Comment on items checked yes!

SUICIDE ASSESSMENT

1. IS SUICIDAL IDEATION PART OF
   THE PRESENTING PROBLEM? ☐ YES ☐ NO

   IS THERE A PLAN? ☐ YES ☐ NO

2. IS A SUICIDE ATTEMPT PART OF THE
   PRESENTING PROBLEM? ☐ YES ☐ NO

3. HAS CLIENT TRIED TO COMMIT SUICIDE? ☐ YES ☐ NO

4. IS THERE A HISTORY OF SUICIDE IN FAMILY
   OR FRIENDS? ☐ YES ☐ NO

5. IS CLIENT HOMICIDAL OR HAVE HISTORY
   OF ASSAULTIVE/VIOLENT BEHAVIOR? ☐ YES ☐ NO

6. IS CHILD ABUSE SUSPECTED?
   ☐ NOT APPLICABLE ☐ YES ☐ NO

7. MANAGEMENT PROBLEM? ☐ YES ☐ NO

7. COMMENTS

1. _____

2. _____

3. _____

4. _____

5. _____

6. _____

7. _____

8. SELF PORTRAIT & FAMILY PORTRAITS

(Give client attached sheets of paper for drawing
and avoid accepting stick figures).

SUMMARY OF MENTAL STATUS EXAM

_____

_____

_____

_____

_____

_____

_____

_____

_____

_____

_____

Therapist Signature: _____

Date: _____

Self Portait

Family Portait

About the Author

HILDEGARD MESSENBAUGH, M.D. is the founding psychiatrist and Program Director of Third Way Center, Inc. She earned her medical degree at the University of Rochester (New York) and completed her residency in adolescent psychiatry at the University of Colorado Health Sciences Center. She was fortunate to work under the late Henry Kempe, M.D. where she gained valuable experience treating children who had endured significant abuse and neglect.

Prior to Third Way Center, she served as the Medical Director of the Adolescent Inpatient Units at the University of Colorado Health Sciences Center and Lutheran West Pines Psychiatric Centers, and developed a thriving private practice in Denver. Her community service includes positions with the Colorado Advisory Council on Mental Health and as commissioner on the Governor's Special Task Force on the welfare of Children.

It is her personal experience, however, that makes her uniquely qualified to treat the teens at Third Way Center. Hildegard's story begins years before she arrived in Denver, as a young child born into a family of wealth shortly before World War II.

Hildegard's family was stuck in the middle. Born in a part of

Yugoslavia, which was shortly thereafter annexed to Hungary. Her family became without a country. Her family roots were two centuries deep in this community. Where her ancestors had carried a German surname and had fallen in love with Hungarians, Christians and Jews. Her family became without an ethnicity. They were not identified as part of the Axis or the Allies, and in the end they discovered they were threatened by both.

As World War II was raging, attacks on neighbors with German surnames forced Hildegard's family to flee in the night to Budapest when she was only four years old. Finding no safety there, the family continued on to Austria, in hopes that their German surname would bring them some security in that foreign land. Unfortunately, Nazis captured the family and sent them to a concentration camp since they were not German and had no country to call home. Miraculously they all survived, and they were abandoned in the countryside with no resources. Hildegard recalls spending the next two years begging for food in the streets until a visa was granted allowing the family to come to the U.S. and begin to rebuild their lives.

Hildegard understands trauma at the core of her being and knows how important it is for each individual to find their own restorative justice for the harm done to them. It is only after achieving this personal justice that an individual is empowered and free to move on. She has had an extraordinary personal journey that has led her to Third Way Center to help thousands of severely abused and neglected adolescents have the opportunity to build a better life. The creation of this philosophy and a lifetime of helping those who couldn't defend themselves is her justice.

Getting Even is an invaluable resource for anyone providing care to traumatized youth and families.

As a clinical psychologist who specializes in childhood grief and trauma, I value the unique contribution of Dr. Messenbaugh's individualized approach to helping traumatized adolescents heal and grow. In a society in which youth manifesting the disruptive sequelae of cumulative trauma and loss are often given up on—with claims they are too far gone to help, Hildegard and her compassionate team at Third Way offer hope and restoration. Their innovative approach to really know and support the whole child within their socioenvironmental context is a reminder that we are all responsible for doing our part to help the youth in our community thrive.

—Brook Griese, Ph.D.
Co-Founder and Executive Director, Judi's House and JAG Institute for Grieving Children and Families

The truth is the world breaks people in unbelievable and unbearable ways. And those of us who are broken hand that hurt on to our kids making sure that trauma continues in a perfect circle.

Hildegard Messenbaugh has proven that, through her work, it is possible to break that cycle of trauma people and build healthy families from our own ruin. She is our great messenger of truth and hope, those two all powerful forces that the world scarcely understands but desperately needs.

—Colorado State Senator Michael Johnston